"Mined
with a Motion"

"Mined with a Motion"

The Poetry of Gerard Manley Hopkins

Marylou Motto

Rutgers University Press
New Brunswick, New Jersey

Publication of this book has been aided by a grant from the National Endowment for the Humanities.

Library of Congress Cataloging in Publication Data

Motto, Marylou, 1946–
 "Mined with a motion."

  Bibliography: p. 189
  Includes index.
   1. Hopkins, Gerard Manley, 1844–1889—Criticism and interpretation. I. Title.
PR4803.H44Z7214 1984   821'.8   83-17844
ISBN 0-8135-1036-8

to my father and mother

199540

Contents

Preface

This book concerns the motions of voice in the poetry of Gerard Manley Hopkins. It argues that Hopkins' poems contain motions of language—discernible patterns—that themselves express the religious affirmation the poetry is talking about. The motions are here called *assent* and *recurrence*.

By motions of assent, I mean the many and varied ways in which Hopkins' voice moves to celebrate the revealed world. By motions of recurrence, I mean the ways in which his voice moves to discover meaning by sighting connections between events in time. Neither motion is absolute, and each has to be made again and again, sometimes at the cost of a strenuous exertion of self.

Hopkins' struggle to enact belief through the motions of assent and recurrence is part of a larger struggle between the secular Romantic world, the dominant culture and aesthetic into which he was born, and the Christian world he elected. Romanticism esteems the individual human imagination, crediting it with the power to shape and even to create its world. But Christianity insists on a God-created world, on the individual's subordination to that God-created world, and on a human life and history directed from without. In choosing a religious life, Hopkins pushed away not only from the Romantic beliefs of his time but from the modes of poetry those beliefs had informed. Assent and recurrence are motions of voice that reach out to affirm an externally determined world.

But these motions are hard-won. The drama of the poetry is in the voice's struggle to approach its prescribed and chosen goal. Hopkins' voice must escape the centripetal forces, turning, breaking through to an offertory verse—dedicated and directed to something outside the self. This drama of direction is central to the poetry, at many times ritualized in its paths and relatively unproblematic, but sometimes freshly contested in the difficulty of poetic creation. The extremes of language in Hopkins' poems accentuate the struggle going on, the stress within the seeking, gesturing voice of the poet. And occasionally, the direction of the voice cannot be held at all. Then, the voice starts to veer off into its own self-concern in which the subordination of self and word begins to be confused and lost.

Won or lost, Hopkins' struggle against the subjective self within a voice so distinctive shapes for the reader essential drama: the self at the world's center, the subordinate world there only for the self's enjoyment, as against the self subordinated—as it finally must be—to its place and time, to a world or a God that controls it and that will necessarily have the last word. In its energetic orality, in its distinctive diction and syntax, in its extreme activity of speech and language, Hopkins' voice is mined with motions that make the reader hear and know this essential struggle as it happens.

The first chapter, "Gestures of Assent," begins with a summary of the ideological and aesthetic opposition between Hopkins and the Romantics. It then explores the directed assent that is a fundamental (and un-Romantic) pattern of activity for the Hopkins speaker, poem, and reader. Last, the chapter looks at a few poems, especially the sonnets of desolation, in which the motions of assent are reversed or wholly lost.

"Lyricism and Design," the second chapter, isolates two kinds of language that Hopkins employs, and it finds some characteristic patterns of their alternation and interaction in the poetry. Within this framework, the chapter then examines some of the ways and places in which Hopkins resists the temptation of an overwhelming lyricism and usually, though not always, manages to counter and direct it with design.

The third chapter, "Bidding," focuses on four characteristic syntactical structures and their close relation to the poet's idea of man's 'calling' in the world. Again, the sonnets of desolation—the poems which came "unbidden"—are seen to be far removed from Hopkins' usual practices and premises, falling into other, more expressionistic syntactical structures.

The fourth chapter, "Dramas of Time and Loss," looks at the temporal modes at work in the poetry and introduces the theme of recurrence, a concept based in the Christian idea of directed time. Recurrence, a continuity made possible by the coming of a savior, denies the absolute isolation of self and moment. But at times in Hopkins, retrospection, imposed on the speaker's chronological time, yields an experienced time so present in and because of the poetry that the poem seems a way of knowing and creating the self.

The last chapter draws on earlier discussions to develop an extended reading of *The Wreck of the Deutschland,* a reading focused on the speaker's relation to his own text and word, explicitly a subject of the poem. Although the poem sets out to 'read' an exterior event in the world, among the various processes enacted, the most essential is tacit: the speaker's poetic creation, an imaginative and interior process continually rising toward and falling away from symbol. Again, drama occurs in the conflict between what the poem ostensibly says and the implicit processes which produce that saying.

As should be clear from these brief and schematic remarks, the book does not focus upon theological issues in Hopkins' poetry but attends to Hopkins' language, assuming that priest and poet are always at issue in a study of Hopkins' poetic voice. Nor does the book work through the Hopkins canon poem by poem. Although some chapters include an extended reading of a single poem or two, the book is more often concerned with fragments of poems, with seeing motions of voice common to many poems, and with seeing the relation between poetic voice and reader. Throughout, I make some use of Hopkins' other writings, especially the reader-oriented prose of the letters, but my main interest is to find what the poems are saying and doing, to essay the essential motions in the activity of their language.

Acknowledgments

It is a pleasure to thank publicly The American Council of Learned Societies and Rutgers University for the time, which grant and fellowship gave me, to revise my work into the present form. To Anthony Hecht, who directed the original thesis from which this book derives, goes my gratitude for his knowledge, time, and care; to Joseph H. Summers, my thanks for his detailed comments and hearty encouragement; to Ann Chalmers Watts, my thanks for her fine delight. My many debts to readers and scholars of Hopkins are specifically acknowledged in the notes to this book.

I would also like to acknowledge permission to cite material from the following:

The Letters of Gerard Manley Hopkins to Robert Bridges, edited by Claude Colleer Abbott. Oxford University Press (1935) on behalf of the Society of Jesus.

The Poems of Gerard Manley Hopkins, edited by W. H. Gardner and N. H. MacKenzie, 4th ed., Oxford University Press (1967).

"Mined
with a Motion"

I

Gestures of Assent

Hopkins is the Victorian whose poetry takes as its subject a basic Romantic concern: the problem of the perceiver in nature. Hopkins' exploration of the self in relation to nature joins him to his Romantic heritage much more firmly than does his youthful preoccupation with loneliness or his early experiments with Keatsian diction. At the same time, unlike other Victorian poets, Hopkins sharply rejects the major tenets of Romanticism, rejects in large part the whole complex variety of Romantic theories of imagination, perception, and creation. While the Romantic wills himself to know the other through a fusion of the self and the other, Hopkins celebrates God-given otherness. In a general sense he shares this posture with seventeenth-century religious poets, who also subordinate the self to the world; but Hopkins forges a speaker who, by his extreme activity of mind and body, enacts a decidedly post-Romantic religious ontology. The speaker makes gestures of assent—dramatic, directed motions of language, consciousness, and physical being—that present, through image and action, Hopkins' idea of man's place in the world.

At the very close of the 1805 *Prelude*, Wordsworth extends the thought that, in a world seemingly incapable of change, the mind of man provides an image of divinity. Through the creative imagination, man's mind may far surpass in beauty the earth it inhabits:

1

Prophets of Nature, we to them will speak
A lasting inspiration, sanctified
By reason and by truth; what we have loved,
Others will love; and we may teach them how;
Instruct them how the mind of man becomes
A thousand times more beautiful than the earth
On which he dwells, above this Frame of things
(Which, 'mid all revolutions in the hopes
And fears of men, doth still remain unchanged)
In beauty exalted, as it is itself
Of substance and of fabric more divine.

(XIII.442–52)

Wordsworth elsewhere names the Mind of Man, "My haunt, and the main region of my song" (*The Recluse*). His poetry goes to nature most for the meditation that nature provokes in him. The natural geography induces a progressive act of consciousness that reflects upon itself as much as it does on nature.[1] That act of consciousness comes to form its own geography—standing, retreating, stopping, tentatively moving forward, and flowing from the past and into the presence of its own perception. Movement through the mind's geography shapes the poetry, and in the mind's ability to know itself through contemplation of nature, Wordsworth finds compensation for the waning of sensory response, for the loss of youth's "dizzy raptures" and "glad animal movements" ("Tintern Abbey"). Both by its process and by its saying, Wordsworth's poetry ennobles the mind of man—if *The Prelude* does develop a myth of nature, says M. H. Abrams, "this is incorporated within a higher and more comprehensive myth of mind."[2]

In the "Preface" to *Lyrical Ballads*, Wordsworth speaks of the poet, who he is and what he does. The Romantic tradition he there initiates elevates the poet at the same time that it insists that the poet's audience is the common man who can and does learn about himself through poetry. Wordsworth starts his well-known definition prosaically enough: The poet "is a man speaking to men." But the passage on the poet's powers then begins to swell, almost in spite of itself, and to overwhelm all the verbal hesitations and qualifications that protest that the poet's experiences

2

and powers are common. Similarly, Wordsworth's frequent meta-
phor of the poet as teacher sometimes pushes beyond the secular
connotations of teacher into another realm when he dwells on
what it is that the teacher teaches. The instruction the poet offers,
as in the passage quoted above, is ambitious indeed. Earlier in
The Prelude, Wordsworth describes the poet and his work in terms
that leave the constraints of common experience far behind:

> deep joy
> From the great Nature that exists in works
> Of mighty Poets. Visionary Power
> Attends upon the motions of the winds
> Embodied in the mystery of words.
> There darkness makes abode, and all the host
> Of shadowy things do work their changes there,
> As in a mansion like their proper home;
> Even forms and substances are circumfused
> By that transparent veil with light divine;
> And through the turnings intricate of Verse,
> Present themselves as objects recognis'd,
> In flashes, and with a glory scarce their own.
>
> *(V.617–29)*

The sense of things sublime, an experience of the transcendence of
man, comes to be closely associated with Romantic poetry. How-
ever significantly Romantic poets differ from each other in creating
or writing about this experience, their similarities loom larger than
their differences when Hopkins is the measure of contrast. To a
greater or lesser degree, the Romantic poet saw himself as set
off and consecrated by his creative abilities. His visionary power
formed his reason for and his obligation to poetic creation. Insti-
tutionalized religious thought is for the most part absent: The
myth of the external design or designer was distant, abandoned.
Deprived of, or liberated from, belief in a commonly recognized
godhead, the poet projected a vision and then credited that vision
with being visionary. The theory of organic form supported a
poetry that grew to trace an unforeseen activity of mind. The poet,
then, was the man who was sometimes more than man, a kind of

sacred being, a priestlike figure who could more readily experience the "something far more deeply interfused" ("Tintern Abbey") and who was charged with the transmission of that experience to other men.

Coleridge writes that the "reader should be carried forward . . . by the pleasurable activity of mind excited by the attractions of the journey itself" (*Biographia Literaria,* 14). The reader of the poem is invited into the journey of mind, asked to share in the poem as a subject of his own reading, and asked to partake, if he be able, in the experience of being the poet, the creator, through his own visionary imagination. Ideally, the reader becomes the perceiver that the poet was, participating in the motion of thought, aspiring to univocality with the speaker.

Much more than the poets who preceded them, the Romantics formulated their values empirically, through their perception of experience. The poem communicates itself "as an experience," a process or journey through the silent power and ambiguous intercourse of river, ravine, and mountain with the mind. The intercourse between the external and the internal within a process of mind yields the open flow of the poem. In such a poetic, values remain open-ended, never to reach a still fixity, itself a kind of poetic death.[3] In Keats' words, the Man of Achievement was "capable of being in uncertainties, Mysteries, doubts, without any irritable reaching after fact & reason" (letter to George and Tom Keats, Dec. 21–27, 1817).

Fact, reason, and a defined system of religious values are of course integral to Hopkins' outlook and poetry. Far from dwelling in or on the creative imagination, the Hopkins poem, like the poems of a much earlier tradition, would de-emphasize the speaker's importance. The poet's voice is highly distinctive, and we are highly conscious of that voice, yet that distinctive voice is forcefully pushed away from the self and directed out into the world: "Look at the stars!" he urges, "look, look up at the skies!" The "Lake poets," Hopkins comments to Dixon, "were faithful but not rich observers of nature."[4] Perhaps within that comment is the idea that the richness or depth of their work did not describe nature so much as it did the self. Hopkins was decidedly not the poet who sought to deify himself or fashion a priestly mission out of his art; his art remained firmly subservient to his religious vocation—he was not the poet-priest but the priest-poet. He subordinates himself to the world. The role of the poet in Hopkins thus distances itself from its Romantic counterparts who would hold that the creative act was responsible for no less than creating the self. "Still, if we care for fine verses," Hopkins writes in a letter to Bridges, "how much more for a noble life!"[5]

To Dixon, the friend who repeatedly regrets Hopkins' lack of publication, Hopkins more than once points out the unseemliness of publication and fame for a Jesuit, whose beauty ought to be within and go unnoticed by the world.[6] Hopkins takes much care in his explanation, and the subject recurs in the letters. The conflict here is between the poet's need to be published and read, and the priest's felt duty not even to chance recognition and fame, a duty that suggested at first that he ought not write at all. Hopkins' destruction of many of his earlier poems; his long 'silence' on entering the order; his taking up poetry again only at the suggestion of a religious superior; and the rather small corpus he finally produced (small for a major poet but perhaps not so small for an often overworked man who defined himself first and primarily as a Jesuit priest)—all these biographical facts have been seen to reflect Hopkins' conflict about writing poetry. Such a conflict was bound to be rather harshly judged by an aesthetic that is still largely Romantic, insisting on the primacy of artistic creation and the ministry of the poet.[7] At the same time, these biographical facts also speak to Hopkins' often reiterated decision about writing poetry: As much as he might value and enjoy it, it was not as important to him as other things in his life.

Moreover, although Hopkins has political concerns and they are sometimes very troubling, he rejects the tradition, most fully realized in the Romantics, that thought of the poet as instrumental in effecting the reformation or transformation of society.[8] Instead, he comes closer to Auden: "Poetry makes nothing happen." For the priest, there was only one thing finally worth making happen. Poetry does not, Hopkins drily suggests to Dixon, make men any better:

> Our Society values, as you say, and has contributed
> to literature, to culture; but only as a means to an end.
> Its history and its experience shew that literature proper,
> as poetry, has seldom been found to be to that end a very
> serviceable means.[9]

Here, both diction and thought measure poetry with a utilitarian
yardstick, and in terms of concrete results, poetry is found wanting.
The wry, pedagogical tone and the periphrasis (itself unusual for
Hopkins) may hint at a need to impose the correct answer on
Dixon's sincere exhortations for Hopkins to publish. But Hopkins
comes to the same answer repeatedly, and the answer is no less
important than the conflict from which it emerges. For Hopkins,
there were simply more important things for him to be doing, and
those things—his ministry, his teaching—were more important
because they might effect something, might bring men closer to
God. While Keats yearned for a life of pure sensation, Hopkins is
regretful but practical about putting poetry aside under the keenly
felt pressure of time. "I cannot in conscience spend time on po-
etry," he writes to Bridges; to Dixon, "In no case am I willing
to write anything while in my present condition: the time is pre-
cious and will not return again and I know I shall not regret
my forbearance."[10]

At least once, Hopkins goes very far indeed in suggesting an
absolute revulsion for the Romantic concept of the imagination.
His own metaphor for the imagination is telling: The imagination
is a hand, an extension of the physical body, that with which we
gesture, touch, and grasp:

> For myself literally words would fail me to express the
> loathing and horror with which I think of it and of man
> setting up the work of his own hands, of that hand
> within the mind the imagination, for God Almighty who
> made heaven and earth.[11]

Hopkins speaks here of the Greek gods as an ignoble mythology.
The Greek gods were not nearly godlike enough to suit Hopkins,
and although a fine classicist, Hopkins wrote no sonnet on Chap-

man's *Homer*. In fact, for all his close analysis and consideration of poetry, Hopkins finished only one poem that explicitly takes poetry as its subject—and that poem, the fine "To R.B.," speaks of the failure of inspiration in his own verse.

Hopkins again betrays his estimation of the worth of writing poetry when he writes to Bridges, who had just moved to a country home: "I should be sorry to think you did nothing down there but literary work: could you not be a magistrate?"[12] Thus, it is not just that the priesthood as a calling conflicts with that exalted Romantic idea of poetry. Even for Bridges, the Victorian derisive of religion, the man for whose poetry Hopkins expresses real esteem, Hopkins holds that words are not enough. Words are neither enough to serve God nor enough to serve man.

For Hopkins, then, poetry is not like religion: Poetry may comment on religion, may express religion, but it could never have become, as it did for Arnold, a substitute for religion or, as it did for Stevens, a "part of the *res* itself."

The world view sprung from Hopkins' religion stands equally apart from the subjectivity of the Romantics. (Hopkins writes that his sonnet says that Purcell's music " 'is none of your d---d subjective rot.' ")[13] For the priest-poet, the coordinates of the universe are sure. The world is an external certainty that needs no perceiver to create it. It is the object itself, and it exists independently of anyone's perception of it. Further: "The saner moreover is the act of contemplation as contemplating that which really is expressed in the object." The world's importance is as "word, expression, news of God,"[14] and that news of God occurs whether the observer wills it so or not, whether the observer sees it or not. Acknowledged or unacknowledged, it is God who legislates the world.

Hopkins, of course, shares much of this world view with religious poets of the seventeenth century, for, by accepting a received explanation for the world, the religious poet, in Helen Gardner's words, "does write in fetters. He writes as a man committed. . . ." What he commits himself to forms the boundaries of his work, the fetters which must define his viewpoint if his art is to remain subordinate, to serve. "Religion," Gardner comments, "is, or appears to be to those who accept it, revelation, something not invented but given."[15]

So in this sense the work of Hopkins shares its 'givens' and has strong ties to the work of Donne, Jonson, and their heirs. Perhaps it is most like the work of George Herbert, who also discovers his poetry in the discovery of God around him.[16] Herbert's poems, even more consciously than Hopkins', form a full exploration of the spiritual life, and Herbert, like Hopkins, is highly conscious of and interested in inventive form. The two poets trace their moments of grace and desolation within a framework of believed truth; both canons are conspicuous in their experimentation with the word and with the poem. Finally, both poets make significant use of the senses to aid in their assent, relying on the world for revelation of God's word.[17] As W. H. Gardner has shown, Hopkins knew and admired Herbert's work, and Hopkins' words sometimes echo the earlier cleric's.[18] It may be useful, then, to pursue the comparison.

For Helen Gardner, the difference between Hopkins and the seventeenth-century poets is primarily one of voice:

> Unconcerned with the idea that a poet expressed his personality, and concerned instead with the aim of giving fitting treatment in an appropriate form to a chosen subject, the poets of the seventeenth century reveal strongly individual personalities and develop strongly individual styles.

Her point about Hopkins is yet more explicit in an examination of "I wake and feel":

> The poem, for all its depth of feeling and the exactness of so much of its phrasing, has a tone of contrivance, of the factitious. Perhaps it is rather too much to ask that a poem on spiritual dereliction should sound 'natural'; but should it sound melodramatic or so deeply self-absorbed?[19]

"I wake and feel" is of course one of the sonnets of desolation, and its feeling derives from the lack of an externally felt order. Still, the reading Gardner offers keenly perceives that Hopkins' individually forged tone is what sets him apart.

8

By contrast, Herbert's poems nearly always fall to a calmness; they like to achieve very firm resolutions. "Where thou dwellest all is neat," Herbert's speaker says to God in "The Familie." The challenge for Herbert is to discover and rest in the neatness, the rich harmony of the world and of the word. As troubled as much of the speaker's experience is, as many trials as he may have to undergo, the Christian reward is never really out of sight.[20] The faithful man finds himself here in a tradition of commonality, of Christian similarity, a context that is sure.

Thus, the movement of Herbert's poetry is consciously toward a 'neatness' and often infused with the humility of a man who has consciously striven to be childlike. The 'child' speaks often in Herbert's work, and his voice is implicitly present even more often. Herbert's speaker becomes God's child, the poetry implies, in order that his congregation, his flock, his readers may follow his example and become children too. That message, rich in bib-lical allusion, achieves in Herbert an elegant simplicity of texture: "Who in heart not ever kneels, / Neither sinne nor Saviour feels" ("Businesse"). The humility, candor, faith, and trust of the *naif* recur, yielding a voice of neatness and virtuous simplicity, a voice both disarming and integral to the poem's sense.

Understatement and conversational rhythms complement the speaker's childlike virtue, as does the thrust, in the "Jordan" poems for example, away from artificial and mannered writing. And Herbert's frequent and extended use of personification and allegory—devices foreign to Hopkins' work—seems also to be re-lated to the narrator's simplicity. One example and result of all of this is that the reception of the soul into the communion of heav-enly love, the culmination of the soul's progress toward God, is rendered by one simple line, a line as understated, allegorical, and plain as could be imagined: "So I did sit and eat" ("Love [III]"). (One might compare Hopkins' vision of that moment, a stunning attempt to catch in words a blinding flash, the ultimate transfor-mation, in "That Nature is a Heraclitean Fire.")

Thus Herbert's poetry, although richly informed,[21] is consciously aimed at the simplest of readers. His voice is not a voice that insists on its selfhood, and we need know little of the poet to read the poems. His system of beliefs, too, largely explains itself

9

within the canon. Although centuries older than Hopkins' poetry, Herbert's work contains few unfamiliar words. The nature he comments on is highly generalized and thus easily recognized too. For the most part, his poetry omits details, proper nouns, and subjective response to idiosyncratic external event. His poetry seems to prune away these inessentials in order to arrive at the simplicity of the common truth. Time and space are but aspects of eternity, the 'I' of the Anglican becoming a symbol, pushing away the particular and relative dimensions of existence in order to reach the universal.[22] In short, the allusive power and tonal control of the poetry are complex, but they are encased in a diction and syntax meant to be easily accessible.

In extreme contrast, Hopkins' use of the explicit, the specific, and the idiosyncratic is pronounced.[23] In Hopkins, the poem *must* realize the tension, almost physically clasping the pied beauties, in order to "Praise him." If in Herbert the specifics of time and space occasionally appear but want to retire from notice, in Hopkins they want most to be felt as splendid manifestations of the act of creation, themselves forming a path to God. Herbert's inessentials are Hopkins' essentials. In Hopkins, the child appears often an object of wonder, and childhood is a time as qualitatively different from adulthood, its perception as wondrously 'clean,' as it is in the Romantics. No less concerned with moralizing dogma than Herbert's speaker, Hopkins' speaker leaves no doubt that his moments of light are fleeting and have to be caught quickly. While both Herbert and Hopkins are directed toward the world, it is Hopkins who tries to seize that world with uncommon physical particularity, whose poetry moves in located time and space, and whose voice more forcefully seeks to define and reach the world as it is here and now. The overt texture of the voice as it struggles with the word and with the world, the knotted and difficult syntax and diction, could not be more different from the texture of Herbert's voice.

The two voices delineate, perhaps, a difference of emphasis between the two traditions, Anglican and Roman Catholic. Yet the two speakers also reflect the historical gap of the two centuries that separate them. For finally, it may well be that the intervention of the Romantics allows Hopkins' voice to occur. In their elevation of the poet and of the individual, the Romantics proclaimed the supreme importance of the self and, more particularly, of the poetic self. Their proclamation fostered a new luxuriance in the ego and took for granted the seriousness of the idiosyncratic—and often rather unmotivated—emotional intensity of the individual. Hopkins, in harking back to an even earlier poetic world view, does so with a voice that relies on the Romantics for strength and acceptance at the same time that his voice rejects the Romantic version of self-importance that gave it being in the first place.

Unlike the Romantic poem, then, the Hopkins poem does not set out to create a world through imaginative perception. It sets out to find the world, to uncover the presence and news that is already there. Robert Langbaum writes that "to know an object, the romanticist must *be* it."[24] In Hopkins, the poet cannot enter or become the object of his attention any more than the reader can escape his own instress (Hopkins' word for the energy which holds a thing together and gives it dynamic individuality but at the same time bodies forth the unifying power behind the world). If, through active attention, the poet can instress the other (for Hopkins uses the word as a verb, too, marking the act of rare perception, an apprehension of instress in the other), it may provoke in him a depth of feeling in response or bring his own instress into the unitive design that includes the other. Unlike Shelley or Keats, however, Hopkins is never under any illusion that he can become the bird—nor does he wish to "cease upon the midnight" when the windhover leaves him behind. For Hopkins, no matter how exciting or intense his sensuous relation to the other, meaning has yet to be discovered, said. Although he can and does move in emotional and mimetic response, in sympathy and partial understanding, he cannot ever really be one with the object of his attention. As he says, "searching nature I taste *self* but at one tankard, that of my own being," and "when I compare my self, my being-myself, with anything else whatever, all things alike, all in the same degree, rebuff me with blank unlikeness."[25] The taste of self must divorce him from the surrounding world. There is no confusion of inner and outer worlds. The other remains the other.[26]

The Hopkins speaker is most often located as an active spectator. For the poems do not present themselves as the poems of genesis; they are, rather, the poems of a creative exegesis—not a Torah, but a Talmud. If the Romantic went outdoors to create the world through his vision, Hopkins, like Herbert, goes out to find God in his creation. In this sense, the poetry, the exegetical uncovering, comes after the fact, after the revelation, and after the cry of the Deutschland's nun. Hopkins' perceived role is to report back, to edit and annotate, to reveal the world, himself, and his poetry by extending the *hand* of the imagination to find the shape and feel of God in the world. This role is not always sustained—perhaps inevitably, the Romantic aesthetic held more allure for Hopkins than his own dogma would grant it—but it is surely Hopkins' most characteristic and pervasive role. The Romantic poet as visionary shaped and created the world through his imagination; the poet as spectator, as commentator, as reader of the world, uncovers the poem's design in the discovery of God's design.

Unlike the Romantic visionary who would create the world, then, the Hopkins speaker goes out to observe and respond to God's creation in the world. The poem details the observation and records and embraces his response of glad appreciation, of assent. In fact, the poem itself is a further response of assent, confirming what has already happened and the continuing presence of God in the world.

Yet such a description of poetry might roughly fit the work of other religious poets. Hopkins is unique in the extent to which he carries his rejection of the exalted, Romantic ideas of the poet and of the interiority of the poem. His response to the world insists on activity, exerting its energy of physical motion, of consciousness, and of language in specific and telling directions that over and over illustrate the proper place of man in the world. The poems both picture and linguistically enact a linear pattern of motion that dramatizes the subordination of self to the real creation and to the ordained goal of man on earth.

The nature of Hopkins' response to the world touches closely on Cardinal Newman's *Grammar of Assent. An Essay in Aid of a Grammar of Assent*, published in 1870, grounds itself in the psychology of response to cognitive and sensual ways of knowing in the world. Newman upholds the primacy of human nature, which disbelieves logical proof at times, yet at other times believes wholeheartedly although it has no scientific basis for belief. According to Newman, man is compelled to believe in religious matters without scientific bases; compelled to give what Newman calls "real assent" (sensuous, intuitive assent as opposed to "notional," or intellectual, assent) because religious propositions do not always have absolute empirical or logical proof. Moreover, such assent without proof of proposition is in no way the weaker response, nor should it be. Just as in life we assent to thousands of everyday ideas, principles, morals, and thoughts without exploring them, so in religion man is fully justified in accepting and assenting to that which his heart tells him is right, whether or not he is cognizant of theological proof of belief. "Life," writes Newman, "is not long enough for a religion of inferences."[27]

Indeed, the assent, "the absolute acceptance of a proposition without any condition," which Newman speaks of depends very little on cognitive understanding. "It is possible to apprehend without understanding," he explains early on. More important than cognitive understanding in real assent is the sensuous transaction between object or experience and self: "As notions come of abstractions, so images come of experiences; the more fully the mind is occupied by an experience, the keener will be its assent to it, if it assents, and on the other hand, the duller will be its assent and the less operative, the more it is engaged with an abstraction."[28] Since it is real assent that appeals to the imagination, it is real assent that is most likely to lead to action.

Hopkins was taken with Newman's work and twice offered, in 1882–83, to write a commentary on the *Grammar*. Newman took Hopkins' assent to his book as the compliment it was but refused the notional commentary.[29] One suspects that Newman had merely confirmed and elaborated what was already in Hopkins' own mind, for in Hopkins' work the validity of sensuous assent is everywhere in force. As early as in an undergraduate essay on Parmenides, Hopkins had written: "But indeed I have often felt when I have been in this mood and felt the depth of an instress or how fast the inscape holds a thing that nothing is so pregnant and straightforward to the truth as simple *yes* and *is*."[30]

For assent is the response possible to the world as news of God. The poet cannot change the world, does not create it with his vision, but he can acknowledge it and the experience of it, can acknowledge what is, its inscape and instress, and clasp it to himself in his heartfelt yes. Similarly, the reader may not be able to achieve univocality with the poem's voice, as he may in Romantic poetry, but he is kept in a ready state of recognition, is kept ready to say yes. The reader apprehends and responds to that response by assent—although the reader may assent primarily not to God in the world but to the poet speaking in the poem. The reader assents through his apprehension of the object of his perception, although not necessarily understanding on a cognitive level; and possibly, because of the need for mystery, the reader necessarily does not understand, but he still rises in response, says yes.

The yes-saying clasps instress, inscape, assents to the assent of the world or of the poem, "Down[s] all that glory." In Hopkins, the description is the praise, the praise is the description, and the more instressed the description, the higher the praise. Assent is an act of mind or body or language moving to meet and confirm feeling. If we know the world to be full of pied beauty, say any number of poems, then the conclusion is inescapable: We *must* "Praise him." The syntax is imperative because the duty is imperative; both the feeling and the response are necessary. If assent does not fully feel the force of the experience, it is bound to be weaker, "notional." Conversely, without the responding assent, feeling remains undirected, purposeless, even chaotic.

So the poem in Hopkins answers experience with the response of assent. The sharpness of the image that fully occupies the mind enables the speaker to discover God and so to shape the keen assent. Indeed, the poems form, in a way, their own grammar of assent in their celebration of God in the world, finding diverse modes and ways of saying that assent—and then often assenting to assent in further and yet stronger response.

The speaker's physical gestures that everywhere occur in the poems are actions, responses, rising instinctively out of real assent.

Physical gestures express the body's strong assent; they are assent. The recognition of God in the world and the litanies and catalogues that that recognition provokes say the poem's assent; what functions first as image for the reader is already assent, the yes-saying response, in the fact of its presence on the page. The speaker's subordination of self to the world is a recognition of larger importance, also an assent to God. As if to reiterate all these things, the speaker sometimes pauses within the poem to affirm the assent he is saying—an emphatic reflexive consciousness that makes the reader all the more aware of the authorial voice behind the speaker: "Í say more:" ("As kingfishers catch fire"); "With witness I speak this" ("I wake and feel"). And finally, even the motion of the poem attests and agrees to Christ's meaning in the world, assents to the idea of direction and goal.

In *The Wreck of the Deutschland*, Hopkins finds himself touched and mastered by a tale of a shipwreck and a nun in that shipwreck who calls to Christ. Before he comes to tell that story, though, Hopkins is drawn to relate a time when he was touched and mastered by God. There is certainty in his telling of his reaction:

> I did say yes
> O at lightning and lashed rod; (2)

The speaker said yes; the captain of the Eurydice said yes; the nun said yes.

The directness of diction in "I did say yes" is clear assent; in fact, the directness expresses a present assent to the previous assent, the time of the original saying. Moreover, characteristically, the "I" is subordinated, becomes the thing which is saying yes.[31] If the Romantic poem seeks to make the object subject, the Hopkins poem seeks to make the subject object, predicating most often a self that is finished, made, and that can itself be perceived as an object in the world:

> the just man justices;
> Keeps gráce: thát keeps all his goings graces;
> ("As kingfishers catch fire")

15

Action is dominant, so the just self, static, is subordinate to its justicing. The justicing, perhaps, *is* the justness—man cannot be just without justicing. 'Keeping' moves beyond its ordinary sense, approaching willed action. And Hopkins wrests meaning from word order as if he were writing in Latin: "all his goings" is 'kept' on the page, surrounded by "keeps . . . graces." The unknowable entity of grace becomes more material and real when it appears in the plural and is identified (by rhythm, sounds, placement) with "goings." Over and again, and in all sorts of ways, Hopkins demystifies and clarifies.

In "I did say yes," speech itself may become gesture. The act of speech is here real act, a motion toward, a literally moving response in assent to past assent. The directness of diction strives to validate the reality of response; that is, language—the clear saying of assent—here externalizes an interior response and grants it factuality, finality. Language becomes gesture.

The interior process seeking expression in the Romantic poem, on the other hand, is an open-ended experience, an experience that escapes precise definition and conclusion, factuality and finality. In Wordsworth, ambiguity and indistinction of syntax reflect the unknownness of what cannot be known, the uncertainty of internal and external placement, the mystery of the object become—or, rather, becoming—subject.[32] In the heightened experiences there, the mind's process knows no material boundaries in its merging of self with other.

Ironically, it is Hopkins, the priest, who makes us aware of the physical. Diction in Hopkins strives most for the hard edge of clarity—distinctness and distinction. Language and structure are used with rigorous precision. What is ordinarily understood as mental process exerts itself in the Hopkins poem through bodily gesture, finding visible outlines, boundaries in time and space within the external world.[33] The action of gesture outlines response in the physical world, gives it parameters, takes response out of its often tacit dimension and realizes it in time and space.

Words are not enough. For Hopkins, the adequate response to God in the world is action, and the whole thrust of the poetry is bent toward action, imaging even nonaction in surprisingly phys-

16

ical terms. Out of the tacit dimension and into time and space, gesture moves in assent to the world:

> I caught this morning morning's minion, king-
> ("The Windhover")

Much of the force of "I caught" arises from the impossibility of literally catching the falcon described. The phrase is an abbreviation of the longer phrase 'I caught sight of,' yet it is surely meant to go beyond the casualness and uncertainty of that phrase; it is surely meant to draw on our sense of the words as Hopkins wrote them—"I caught." The poet's "hand within the mind" reaches out to do the seeing, turns seeing into an active moving of the self toward another movement. Indeed, in the energetic particularity of the description that follows, it seems not merely his eye which has caught the windhover but his whole self moving in response:

> My heart in hiding
> Stirred for a bird,—

Formlessness, obscurity, the heart still and quiet in its enclosure, all become distinct in the motion to escape that enclosure, to move out toward the world in gesture. "In hiding" restrains, holds back, the line, hesitates there in the hush of the alliterated '*h*'s,' marking time before the strong stress and long length of the syllable "stirred," which emphatically marks the turning of the verse. And then the rhyming of "stirred" with "bird" daringly pulls the motion toward its object, both words strongly drawing away from "My heart" and so subordinating the heart to the motion it enacts. Poetic rhythm mimes the action of the heart pushing out against its enclosure, becoming physical and active, in "stirred."

At the same time, the language that mimes the heart's stirring means to be subordinate to that stirring, the original real response in the world. In "Brothers," Hopkins tells the story of two young boys. Jack, the younger boy, is on stage and "bráss-bóld," something of a ham—"Dog, he did give tongue!" Harry, in contrast to Jack, is positioned against a wall and apprehensive about his brother's showing on stage. In his nervousness, Harry smiles, blushes, bites his lips, clutches his fingers, can't bring himself to watch, and finally, at Jack's success, buries his tear-stained face in his hands, "For fond love and for shame." In other words, the boy who performs on stage gives "tongue," speaks his part, and so gains loud, public applause, but Harry—like Hopkins' Alphonsus Rodriguez, a quieter soul—has far more to communicate and communicates far more without speech. For Hopkins, the real drama is in Harry: Harry's response is the deeper and more affecting precisely because it uses no words but emerges in action, in the spontaneous gestures of love.

In "Spring and Fall," too, the child's wordless tears compel the speaker's attention and response because they emerge from the heart and are not filtered through the feeble, distorting medium of language: "Nor mouth had, no nor mind, expressed / What heart heard of, ghost guessed." For Hopkins, as for other poets and most especially the Romantics, language is always inadequate to experience; but Hopkins finds and values a whole other vocabulary of communication when he details so many gestures, figures meaning in gestures, and so consistently celebrates the moving self in language.

In another instance, Hopkins makes conversion literal, an active turning:

> And fled with a fling of the heart to the heart of the Host.
> My heart, but you were dovewinged, I can tell,
>   Carrier-witted, I am bold to boast,
> To flash from the flame to the flame then, tower from the grace
>   to the grace.
>
> *(Deutschland, 3)*

The "dovewinged" heart flung and flashed and towered, and only now, in the speaking of the poem, does the speaker tell and boast, use language. The poem is subordinate to the event of the heart's motion; the poem proves a true, if intellected, further assent, but always with reference to the real assent that needed no words. The action is dazzling here, the "I" seemingly tied to the heart which quite literally ran away with it.

In fact, the use of "heart" throughout the poetry exemplifies Hopkins' gesture-making. It shows his habit of attributing physical reality, will, and motion, to what we ordinarily think of as invisible, mysterious, or incorporeal. So the speaker grants his heart a separate but equal existence, or even a dominant one:

> Heart, go and bleed at a bitterer vein . . .
> > *(Deutschland, 3 1)*

> My héart, where have we been?
> > ("St. Winefred's Well," *Act II*)

These are more than personifications. Hopkins is here taking the old clichés—that our hearts are moved, that they move us—and making them literal, real. If the Romantic would make us know the mystery within, Hopkins would have us see the clarity. Heart becomes a real presence in the poetry precisely because it is so often on its own, physically gesturing in response to the world.[34]

In "Morning, Midday, and Evening Sacrifice," Hopkins couples the heart with parts of the body we are used to seeing and moving:

> Both thought and thew now bolder
> And told by Nature: Tower;
> Head, heart, hand, heel, and shoulder
> That beat and breathe in power—

The alliteration of the stressed nouns says, as the list itself says, that the heart is as tangible and knowable as its partners. In "Hurrahing in Harvest," Hopkins physically images the 'raising' of his spirits:

> I walk, I lift up, I lift up heart, eyes

Everything conspires to make us see and feel an actual uplifting here: the pairing of "heart" and "eyes"; the progressive lengthening of the parallel clauses; the strong stresses on the last two nouns; the subordinated but repeated "I" turning into the expan-

19

sive, commanding "eyes" with its trailing 's' sound after all the
earlier stopped noun endings.

But even more often than it is paired with other things, the
heart in Hopkins strikes out on its own. In "Carrion Comfort"
the heart's actions mark a turning point of the poem when the
speaker comes to realize that his remembered agony was not as
desperate or as comfortless as he had thought at the time:

> Nay in all that toil, that coil, since (seems) I kissed the rod,
> Hand rather, my heart lo! lapped strength, stole joy, would
> laugh, chéer.
> Cheer whom though?

The heart is the agent of the interchange: It starts out almost
unnoticed in its shy and even furtive actions (lapping, stealing)
but ends in a fine and firm happiness that denies despair, a happi-
ness that may even have cheered its maker (in *both* senses—'made
happy' *and* 'applauded,' a wholehearted gesture of assent).

Through imaged gestures, then, the heart's motions become the
man's emotions and vice versa. The subject of directional force in
Hopkins' poetry will recur, but it is worth noting now that the
heart's motions are literally e-motions, moving away from, out
from, the self. The traditional seat of man's essential goodness,
the enclosure of enclosures, breaks open under the pressure that
Christ brings to bear and so realizes man's hidden potential in
visible action, knowable gesture. At its most profound level, the
idea of this signal event stands behind all of Hopkins' poetry,
for the heart breaking open is the poet's figure for the salvation
of man:

> The dense and the driven Passion, and frightful sweat:
> Thence the discharge of it, there its swelling to be,
> Though felt before, though in high flood yet—
> What none would have known of it, only the heart, being hard
> at bay,
>
> Is out with it!
>
> *(Deutschland, 7–8)*

20

Alone, enclosed, bereft of communication, the heart may "grate on" itself ("Patience, hard thing!"), become haggard ("The Golden Echo"), or burn ("I wake and feel"); but when Christ takes it on, when it is countered from without and driven to respond, something else again occurs. In the passage quoted above, the heart ('hart') is cornered and driven, its back against the waters. It alone now breaks, replies to Christ's passion, "Is out with it!" If that exultant ending does not precisely define what the heart's gesture is in concrete terms, it does most clearly express the fact of the gesture, the direction and speed of it, and its breathtaking value. At the critical moment, "only the heart" leaps to the response, the instinctive gesture, which alone can save man.

Gesture, whether of heart or body, is an illustration and emblem of the mind's assent, but it also serves in the poem to authenticate that assent. Gesture makes what is fluid hard and knowable. In its turning of thought or emotion into act, gesture turns thought into verifiable fact. It realizes the self in the world and so ends the circularity of interminable interior motion. The Romantic creative imagination is in its ultimate degree an enclosure, seeking to subsume the world within the self, implicitly proclaiming 'I am that I am.' In the Hopkins poem, gesture as assent, gesture *and* assent, break out of such enclosure of the self to reach for and point at the world, proclaiming, as they reach, 'I am that he made me.' Gesture is a mode, a most powerful mode, of tendering "beauty, beauty, beauty, back to God."

Conceptually, the Hopkins poem starts where many lyrics start— in the noticing of, the pointing toward, something in the world. But that notice remains based in the visual and does not lead to the wholly inner meditation that gathers world into mind. The enclosing process of the Romantic creative imagination moves man toward a world that asks a minimum of physical action, a solipsistic environment in which the world's otherness seeks to be mediated and even absorbed. In this, and in its purposeful confusion of time sense, the Romantic creative imagination posits a world without Christ, a world without direction or final meaning, a confusion of boundaries that has no sense of beginning or end, of linearity.[35] The Hopkins poem, however, seeks out the sharpness of the world's objects, catches the clarity and distinctness that force man to attend to the reality outside of himself. It may even be that the "heart right" (*Deutschland,* 29) must respond in direction, gesture, and action, in order to *be* the "heart right." The "heart right" *must* come "out with it!"

Hopkins explains that the whole world gives glory to God but that only man can intend to do so:

> The sun and the stars shining glorify God. They stand where he placed them, they move where he bid them. 'The heavens declare the glory of God'. They glorify God, *but they do not know it.* The birds sing to him, the thunder speaks of his terror, the lion is like his strength, the sea is like his greatness, the honey like his sweetness; they are something like him, they make him known, they tell of him, they give him glory, but they do not know they do, they do not know him, they never can, they are brute things that only think of food or think of nothing. This then is poor praise, faint reverence, slight service, dull glory. Nevertheless what they can *they always do.*
>
> . . . But man can know God, *can mean to give him glory.* This then was why he was made, to give God glory and to mean to give it; to praise God fréely, wíllingly to reverence him, gládly to serve him. Man was made to give, and mean to give, God glory.[36]

Charged with the grandeur of God, the world "will flame out": That "will" partakes of both the indicative and the imperative mood. It *will* flame out, it will fulfill its being, go itself. The human self, however, is allowed on some level to choose whether or not to act as it was meant to act. God charges man to indicate this charge, to glorify God. So, it is man's free will—what Hopkins calls the *arbitrium*—that can win him heaven. In the indication, in the clarity of freely willed response to the world's clarity, assent—and not the creative imagination—defines the self. Gesture, its sign, breaks out of the solipsistic environment, pushing onward and outward, attesting to a meaningful universe, a goal and end to life, a Christ-informed world.

It does this because gesture possesses directional, volitional force.[37] It is movement away from one thing, the enclosure of the self, and toward another, the world. Without direction, the self is purposeless, and both body and beauty are doomed, decaying. The self that seeks stasis becomes the self tragically trapped in a dying animal; the enterprise is futile for man cannot be autonomous, self-enclosed:

>   since, no, nothing can be done
> To keep at bay
> Age and age's evils, hoar hair,
> Ruck and wrinkle, drooping, dying, death's worst, winding
>   sheets, tombs and worms and tumbling to decay;
> So be beginning, be beginning to despair.
> O there 's none; no no no there 's none:
> Be beginning to despair, to despair,
> Despair, despair, despair, despair.
>
>   ("The Leaden Echo")

To seek to hold back mortal beauty is to choose to hoard the self and stay time; prideful and futile, the act can lead only to despair. The gesture that moves out of the self, however, intimates a self back on the line of Christian time, for gesture has goal, suggests meaning and purpose, exists in and toward the world. With its body, shape, and bearing, in its visible beginning and end, gesture assents to man's power and free will at the same time that it defines man's limits and boundaries in time and space. The grandeur of God "will flame out," and the repeated gestures of the poem, like heart in *The Deutschland,* all seek to come "out with it!"

The alternative—to be satisfied with enclosure, to cease following traces of God in the world—foregoes direction and force and assents to a lack of meaning:

> Lovely the woods, waters, meadows, combes, vales,
> All the air things wear that build this world of Wales;
>   Only the inmate does not correspond:
>   ("In the Valley of the Elwy")

In contrast to the kind people the speaker remembers (figured earlier as a nesting brood of birds), the "inmate," who lacks grace, cannot wear the world's air (and Hopkins means this "air" *as* air, means it literally as well as in the sense of attitude). The prisoner cannot push out yonder. He cannot wear the world because he dwells "indoors," does not deal himself out, and so has no gesture worth recording. There are other images of destructive enclosure in Hopkins, but perhaps the most interesting are those which refer to man's enforced enclosure, his physical limits as man. Like the caged skylark, man's spirit is pent within an inescapable and burdensome house. Yet in the afterlife, that house—a "bone-house, mean house"—will be no more constricting than the rainbow's weight on the field:

> Man's spirit will be flesh-bound when found at best,
> But uncumberèd: meadow-down is not distressed
> For a rainbow footing it nor he for his bónes rísen.
>
> ("The Caged Skylark")

Part of the poem's assent in Hopkins inheres in the process of the poem itself, for the poems are strongly moved as well as moving, strongly directed. The poem moves outward too. The poem is propelled into the world, where it joyfully takes on the encounter of the swirl of experience, but is also driven to go beyond that ongoing-ness of the world into a more human and conscious going, a more purposed or intellectual or cognitive act of assent to the God-given power of men to give glory. In "As kingfishers catch fire," "Í say more" explicitly marks one such transition point, the poem emphatically pointing at its own development and driving force. For the most part, the direction of the poems seems sure, and the poem imposes itself firmly as product as well as process. The assent of description, in all its energy, signals the imminence of other motion, further motion, a moving yonder. Geoffrey Hartman has commented that in Hopkins "*the act of sight has become a moral responsibility.*"[38] (Note that seeing is an *act*—an act of assent.) But there is more to be gained from attention held, from seeing, for attentiveness may yield a cognitive understanding, the affirmation of assent, or what Newman calls "certitude," the assent to assent.[39] In a notebook Hopkins discusses memory, understanding, and will in terms of temporal progression. Memory projected into the future constitutes imagination; into the past, memory; in the present tense, memory constitutes "attention . . . the being *ware*":

> When continued or kept on the strain the act of this faculty is attention, advertence, heed, the being *ware*, and its habit, knowledge, the being *aware*. Towards God it gives rise to *reverence*, it is the sense of the *presence* of God. The understanding, as the name shows, applies to words; it is the faculty for grasping not the fact but the meaning of a thing. . . . when it [memory] keeps on the strain ('attendere, advertere, et contemplari') it cannot but continuously beget it.[40]

At the right pitch, attention must beget understanding; the yielding of the one to the other is a characteristic pattern in Hopkins.

The Romantic poem centers itself in retrospection, in the meditative pull of past experience that intermingles and fuses, colors and shapes, all experience thereafter. In "The Solitary Reaper," for example, the highland girl seen and heard in the present tense turns out to be a vision from the past, a vision reaped again and again. The conclusion of Wordsworth's poem turns back in on its own turning:

> I listened, motionless and still;
> And, as I mounted up the hill,
> The music in my heart I bore,
> Long after it was heard no more.

The end of this poem sees the mind that has enclosed the experience turn back in on the listening to perpetuate it yet further. The poem seeks to stay time and space. The mind seeks to subsume the world. Music internalized is stilled and silenced, becoming a place of mysterious refuge—just as the girl herself was stilled, 'beheld.' And the poem in its movement inward constitutes another immutable chalice, this time for the reader to bear.

Wordsworth's transference of experience from the highland girl to the speaker to the reader (each is a "solitary reaper"), with its implication that indistinction and retrospection merge subject and object, is in sharp contrast to Hopkins' insistence on distinction and immediacy. The Hopkins poem is firmly grounded in the here and now, tensed in the present. When the memory of differentiated past does occur—as in "Felix Randal" for instance—it becomes a means of moving the present forward; speaker and poem finally stop at a point where they had not before been. The poem seems to know that it is going, moving, and it moves certain in its direction if not in its end. An end is usually in sight. While the closures in Hopkins leave no doubt that they are complete, the sense often seems to be poised on the brink of some yet further and more wondrous finding. Perhaps the fact that the poem is constantly moving into yet further and firmer levels of assent suggests that the poem could continue, could yet move "yonder," beyond itself. And perhaps only a total assent could be a real stopping place for Hopkins, an ultimate act not to be had on earth.

Finally, the movement outward from the self through gesture imparts a fierce dynamism to the speaker and to his spoken word. The gestures that fill Hopkins' poems encourage us to see both the speaker and his word as made objects, actors subordinate to the goal for which they are so enthusiastically reaching out. For the reader, the speaker's gesture is another event, a sighting like the sighting of the falcon, but one which insists on visibly distinguishing itself and on making visibly distinct its otherness. (The speaker *means* his gesture.) For the reader, gesture sharply defines the speaker as the 'other' toward whom he, the reader, is turned. And finally, through its sense of purpose, of speed, and of linearity, the poem itself moves into the realm of gesture and assent and, residing there, serves to make us again aware of the keen outline of otherness.

Tempering the motion outward in gesture, the forceful willed motions into the world, is an impulse that intimately cherishes the other toward whom Hopkins' speaker is turned. In moments of intimacy, the language suddenly softens and slows, relieving the driving, directional force of the poem, as it suggests a drawing in of the other to the speaker's self. There is, momentarily, an intimation of equilibrium, a pause in which the stress of conflicting difference is relaxed:

> No wonder of it: shéer plód makes plough down sillion
> Shine, and blue-bleak embers, ah my dear,
>   Fall, gall themselves, and gash gold-vermilion.

("The Windhover")

Critics have differed about whether "ah my dear" addresses Christ or windhover.[41] The ambiguity, intimating something internal that escapes precise definition, is significant. Drawn to a participation in the event, the speaker breathes "ah my dear" in a contemplative sharing that seems to encompass in its address the bird, Christ, the sillion, the embers, and himself. He treats himself as object, motions in his words with a tenderness toward the self that has found the meaning of the experience undergone and is about to say what he has found: the brilliance revealed at the heart of the blue-bleak embers already named. (Hopkins names this breaking open under intense stress 'selving.') The speaker's self, predicated in the "I" that "caught" the windhover and in the "heart" that "stirred," is at the end of the poem gently greeted as part of the speaker's "dear." And as the self becomes "dear," as the voice says, "ah my dear," a kind of ancillary selving occurs. The "ah my dear" yields up the self even as it accepts and embraces the self; the phrase balances there in its open and trailing sounds before the image— the embers—completes itself in its apocalyptic selving as the voice, the speaker, cannot. The speaker does achieve a kind of participation: "ah my dear" is an action of assent, but it is mortal and therefore incomplete. As "O my chevalier!" addresses and embraces the loveliness born of the sacrifice of Christ and falcon, "ah my dear" similarly, intimately, yields up the self that has seen and read the analogies of Christ and the world. But the intimacy held does not last and cannot last. In the final line of the poem, the speaker moves on descriptively to complete the image of the embers in their ultimate and complete selving: The differentiation between the self and the world is again manifest.

In other places, intimacy is less problematic but no less dramatic. Defined object and self share something or become reciprocal in the motions of language that suggest intimacy. The word 'dear' is often used in these moments to refer to man, object, or abstract. The word comes, in the reading of Hopkins, to be stressed, instressed; we look to it for moments of tenderness upon which the poem lingers. Thus, in "God's Grandeur," "There lives the dearest freshness deep down things" seems to 'spring' the poem's tone far beyond what has gone before and suggest the feeling of intimacy for the living earth underfoot.

In "Felix Randal," the intimacy is even more marked:

This seeing the sick endears them to us, us too it endears.
My tongue had taught thee comfort, touch had quenched thy
    tears,
Thy tears that touched my heart, child, Felix, poor Felix
    Randal;

Priest and blacksmith draw toward one another in "endears," a word that makes gesture or action out of the adjective of relationship. In his fine article on this poem, Joseph Eble says that the first of these lines has a "palindrome effect."[42] Language and sense are reciprocal here, and the line suggests the two men moving toward one another in mutual embrace. Even here, as Hopkins speaks to tender feeling, the poetry reaches for the physical reality that can be seen. The speaker names Felix repeatedly; not language but the visible tongue teaches comfort; by drawing on the previous, literal touch that quenched tears, 'touching the heart' approaches physical action and physical object.

The words of intimacy seem to happen often in apposition—"ah my dear," "O my chevalier," "child, Felix, poor Felix Randal." Will and energy and force as previously known are infused by a deeper force rising within, changing time into experience, and suspending the driving force of referential meaning. Intimacy seems the closest one can come to knowing a single other, and it gives rise to lines and phrases extraordinary for their feeling of breathlessness or tenderness of experience. Such moments are all the more wondrous and dramatic because their gathering in happens within lines and poems that are elsewhere insisting on motion outward and forward. That motion always reasserts itself, for in Hopkins, intimacy is not ultimate knowledge, and it is not meant to be final assent. It is not an end in itself but something that happens in apposition to larger movements.

For Keats, once the discrete experience of intimacy is lost, reality becomes pale, a cold hill side, and Wordsworth would sustain his experience of the girl's song for life. But the Hopkins speaker even in his wonder at what is happening tells us he knows it cannot last. Nor should it. For Hopkins, the intimate experience is but a road to the larger reality that restores subordination and places the self and the other into the larger context. Neither is the human inability to sustain intimacy the tragedy for Hopkins that it is for Arnold; Hopkins wills himself to be true to something that is beyond mere human love. So, what may be intimate knowledge of Margaret allows the speaker to move far beyond Margaret. And the tenderness of the 'embrace' in "Felix Randal" is not discrete event, or not merely discrete event but prelude to a more objective and finally more important motion on both their parts. Felix became the child in order to soar above his teacher; the priest once moved in a tenderness that allows him now to divine that flight. The poem, informed by the intimacy with another, moves back out into the world. It has promises to keep.

B esides the motion out into the world, there is yet another dominant movement in the poems, and this second movement has even closer affinities with assent. Assent, the saying of yes, finds its human and poetic expression most often in a rising of self, an *ascent* or striving upward toward God in body and spirit.

Hopkins is forever looking up—and telling his reader to look up—at what is happening above his head:

> Look at the stars! look, look up at the skies!
> O look at all the fire-folk sitting in the air!
> ("The Starlight Night")

The metaphor of "fire-folk" might bring the stars firmly down to earth by making them familiar and concrete, but Hopkins counters that descent by insisting on the physical gesture of our looking up and by an enthusiasm that would 'lift' us. In a fragment, "Ashboughs," the speaker points to a tree whose boughs "touch heaven, tabour on it," and explains:

> . . . it is old earth's groping towards the steep
> Heaven whom she childs us by.

In Hopkins, both man and nature repeatedly aspire to the "steep / Heaven." Vertical motion serves as figure for the attempt to reach God.

It is true that relatively little in nature happens at eye level, nor do I mean to suggest that Hopkins ignores horizontal movement—"the racing lambs too have fair their fling." But it is vertical movement that most distinguishes its own meaning and captures Hopkins' attention. When he looks down, it is to see weeds shooting up; when he looks up, it is to see the windhover swooping down, or to see nature ascending far above his head, or to see Christ descending in response. The poem "Spring" images the weeds shooting up from the ground, hears the thrush flying, sights the air descending through the ascending leaves and blooms, the lambs flinging, and more. And the transitions *between* the motions of the objects in the world quicken the poem and add to its activity because the object of the speaker's attention changes so rapidly. The speaker shifts eyes, head, and body in an attempt to see it all—or so we feel—and shifts so quickly and decisively as to make us aware of his movement even when he is not explicitly naming directions or saying, "look up at the skies!"

Like nature, the "heart right" bounds out *and* up. "Hurrahing in Harvest" is "the outcome of half an hour of extreme enthusiasm," according to Hopkins:[43]

> Summer ends now; now, barbarous in beauty, the stooks rise
> Around; up above, what wind-walks! what lovely
>   behaviour   2

Of silk-sack clouds! has wilder, wilful-wavier
Meal-drift moulded ever and melted across skies?   4

I walk, I lift up, I lift up heart, eyes,
Down all that glory in the heavens to glean our Saviour;   6
And, éyes, heárt, what looks, what lips yet gave you a
Rapturous love's greeting of realer, of rounder replies?   8

And the azurous hung hills are his world-wielding shoulder
Majestic—as a stallion stalwart, very-violet-sweet!—   10
These things, these things were here and but the beholder
Wanting; which two when they once meet,   12
The heart rears wings bold and bolder
And hurls for him, O half hurls earth for him off under his
  feet.   14

"I lift up" is complete in itself, the elevation named, as well as being an anticipation of the further response, "I lift up heart, eyes." The speaker lifts up heart, eyes, and self to bring back, to "down" glory. And the Saviour, in and of the clouds, himself gestures in return, a lover bending and kissing, responding and touching, because of the speaker's lifting. That the interchange happens once seems to make it possible for it to happen again, and with more force, and the whole process feeds the gradual intensification of the recurring experience. Words and phrases, whole in themselves in their meaning and syntax, are repeated and added to, not only in line five, as noted above, but in lines seven, eight, eleven, thirteen, and fourteen. The speaker is "hurrahing," cheering more and more strongly in response, and "in harvest," literally *in* harvest, his own harvest of nature, of Christ in nature, and of a grace that is his for the exuberant reaching up for it.

The poem is strewn with "*w*'s" and "*h*'s" and nowhere more so than in the concluding sestet, where the sounds suggest the breathlessness of the encounter as the speaker's excitement grows. As Christ winnows and wins the youth in "Spring," he here husbands and gleans the speaker in harvest when the speaker has himself begun to put on Christ's power: The speaker "rears wings bold and bolder / And hurls for him, O half hurls earth for him off under his feet" through the enthusiasm of love. In the moment of encounter, in the 'here' and 'now' of summer's end, ripeness is all. When the meeting does not occur, it is the beholder that is "wanting." That is, he is not there, he is missing from the scene, but also, implicitly, he is "wanting,"—lacking the energy of sight, of faith, of daring—lacking the willingness to look up.

In the *Deutschland,* the speaker looks and gestures upward and is similarly rewarded when Christ answers from the sky:

> I kiss my hand
> To the stars, lovely-asunder
> Starlight, wafting him out of it; and
> Glow, glory in thunder;
> Kiss my hand to the dappled-with-damson west: (5)

Here, the speaker offers a motion of tenderness, the response of assent to the loveliness of the light, and Christ answers him by again bringing home to him himself, making him "Glow, glory in thunder." The answer, wafted by the kiss out of the starlight, embodies the brightness and glory of the stars in the speaker himself: He glows at and in the response. The glow, which is at once his answer from Christ and back to Christ, is itself encircled within the lines by the speaker's kisses in further response, motions of ascent and assent. The syntax thus attempts to enact in language a reciprocal movement, the movement of love at once given and taken and returned to augment the further giving.

"The Leaden Echo" is caught in a dulling stasis that ends in despair. "The Golden Echo" finds within that word "despair" the "Spare!" that is its first verse. But the true contrast to leaden despair comes at the end of the second poem, in parallel position to "despair":

> —Where kept? do but tell us where kept,
> where.—
> Yonder.—What high as that! We follow, now we follow.—
> Yonder, yes yonder, yonder,
> Yonder.

The true contrast and remedy to leaden despair is the golden movement that escapes the self to follow the true keeper of beauty yonder. "What high as that! We follow, now we follow," the speaker promises. Man is mortal, earthbound, and so ascent must always end in descent. The gesture of yes must return to the self, just as it arose out of the self. But it pushes out and up again and again in defiance of its own mortality, in its striving to reach what is necessarily beyond and above its grasp.

So each time the speaker's eyes rise with joy or anticipation, it is a figure, a reminder, of a larger rising, a more strenuous striving of the whole self for what it cannot yet attain. The striving upward in moments of grace may be met by a mastering God, and then, doomed to fail, it fails and falls as it must, but it falls with heroism and shining and grace. The self unselves, seems to shed part of its mortal coil, and gleams in this fall: The coals gash gold-vermilion; the falcon, buckling, breaks into fire. The motion of upheaval, most beautiful and most dangerous when it happens in man, finds external expression for Hopkins in the natural world, in nature, whose dazzling surfaces always want to reflect the possibility of an inner and spiritual analogue in man. The moments in which man reaches for the heavens are moments that call him out of himself, when the unselving of self and escape from the taste of alum are most nearly achieved. Thus, Margaret's spring of empathy and grief makes her tears fall. Felix Randal's bright flight to God happens when his "big-boned and hardy-handsome" body falls apart in his dying. And "honour is flashed off exploit," inner or outer, inner *and* outer.

The ship the Deutschland is powerfully directed in space:

> On Saturday sailed from Bremen,
> American-outward-bound, (*12*)

> Into the snows she sweeps,
> Hurling the haven behind, (*13*)

> She drove in the dark to leeward,
> She struck—not a reef or a rock
> But the combs of a smother of sand: night drew her
> Dead to the Kentish Knock; (*14*)

The movement outward, away from the familiar, is dramatically stopped, broken. As the ship goes down in the midst of the confusion of the storm, the nun breaks open, selves into words that fly *up* to Christ, seemingly presaging her own assumption. More literally than any other selving in the poetry, the nun's assent is an ascent.

The unselving in upheaval is a finding of realer self, a shedding and shelving of what makes man basely mortal, to discover another kind of humanity, the best of what is within him. It is nearly always figured in images of rising and falling. Assent seeks to rise in spite of the fact that its fall is inevitable, for such a fall, painful or happy, is a fortunate one.

The poems are staged in a way that makes these motions clear. Since "with a companion the eye and the ear are for the most part shut and instress cannot come," the poetic speaker is often alone, in nature, where we follow his line of attention.[44] But when Hopkins does use more than one person in a poem, he places them spatially so that one is higher than the other or others.[45] In "Spring and Fall," the speaker looks down fondly at the child, Margaret, from his higher perspective; he looks down, too, at Harry in "Brothers." Harry, who goes through a minor unselving of his own, looks up at his younger brother, John, on stage. In "The Handsome Heart," the speaker looks down to ask a question of a child who, rising to respond, is himself answered by the speaker's admiration. (Like Harry, this child gains stature, 'rises' in the speaker's eyes.) Nor are the characters so positioned always children. The Deutschland nun towers over her peers. The priest tends to Felix Randal, unconverted, in bed but later thinks of the farrier in his earlier stance, rising larger than life at the forge, a stance now spiritually realized in his rising to God. The soldier whom Christ leans down to admire and other working and fighting men also seem larger than life. In fact, whenever he speaks of physical strength or beauty in the poems, Hopkins seems to be literally as well as figuratively looking up to it. Surely much of this admiration for size and strength emerges from Hopkins' belief or hope that they hold the possibility of yet more significant gesture, of larger and more forceful action. (Christ himself is to return as a soldier.) Spatial placement, then, helps to comment on a character's spiritual stance or movement and often serves as symbol for it. Also important, though, is the fact that the stances again focus attention on the *activity* of sight. The spectator-speaker is not passive, is not acted upon, but again has willed head and body toward the object of his attention. Attention itself seems a more physical, directional, volitional response in these poems: Attention approaches gesture. Finally, and predictably, the stances have yet one more effect. As they differentiate characters in vertical space— as well as in horizontal space—the unique otherness of the object of attention is again defined, differentiated, and made manifest.

Thus, the motions of assent, motions outward and upward, are dominant images in Hopkins, figuring a spiritual as well as physical outgoing-ness, a giving off and up of self. But—less frequently to be sure—Hopkins also images dissent, a refusal, willed or unwilled, to extend the hand of the imagination and so see and respond to God's creation. The images of dissent are first associated with mankind in general but then, more complexly, with the speaker himself.

The Hopkins speaker, particularly in the early poems, spends most of his time and energy out of doors—away from man-made constricting enclosures. Clearly, the natural setting is the place where the sense of God in the world is most accessible. But nature is also the place that provides the visual equivalent of a spiritual expansiveness, the place where he, like the Romantics, is most free to 'soar.' Figuratively and physically, and both in terms of stimulus and response, nature invites assent.

Thus, that the response of assent is not always forthcoming from man in nature is a recurring problem to him. The question is posed explicitly, starkly, and forcefully, in "God's Grandeur": "The world is charged with the grandeur of God. . . . Why do men then now not reck his rod?" Characteristically, nay-saying gestures deliberately point downward first and remain stuck to earth. As if in defiance of the heavens above, the gestures of dissent remain willfully shortsighted. They often occur when Hopkins speaks of man's abuse of the world lent to him:

Generations have trod, have trod, have trod;
   And all is seared with trade; bleared, smeared with toil;
   And wears man's smudge and shares man's smell: the soil
Is bare now, nor can foot feel, being shod.

The repetition of "have trod" imitates the insistent and wrong-headed stubbornness of indistinguishable generations of mankind. Man's actions grind down earth and ruin the beauty of earth's otherness, wearing down its selfhood and destroying the full glory it was meant to give. In "Ribblesdale," man deals the "lovely dale down" with the same careless unconcern:

                         —Ah, the heir
To his own selfbent so bound, so tied to his turn,

To thriftless reave both our rich round world bare
And none reck of world after, this bids wear
Earth brows of such care, care and dear concern.

In "Binsey Poplars," the "airy cages" of the trees are "All felled, felled, are all felled"; man has again destroyed God's design and beauty without consideration for what he is doing. That he does such things carelessly betrays his tragic lack of attention to God, to the world lent to him, to the generations to follow, and finally, perhaps primarily, to himself. In willful ignorance, in stubborn concentration on endless self-gratification, the eyes of man descend, remain fixed to the ground, and so image the destructive gesture of willed dissent.

What of the speaker's dissent? In the early and middle periods of Hopkins' poetry, the dissent is mankind's and not the single man's. The accumulation of mankind's 'no' is diametrically opposed in these poems to the speaker's extreme exuberance of 'yes.' But perhaps even before encountering the sonnets of desolation and their terrible, limitless falls, the reader senses the possibility of deep darkness and destruction in a voice so intent on witnessing the world so intensely.

The fall in the sonnets of desolation is a motion that is perhaps a more complete opposite to assent than the simple, willed dissent already discussed, for in the sonnets of desolation the speaker's movements are often internal and unwilled. The experience of deep interiority, an experience the Romantics cultivate and celebrate, terrifies Hopkins. In these poems, the speaker cannot escape the hell of his own self and becomes a helpless subject of forces beyond his control. If the willed gestures drastically diminish, the images themselves seem at times to be flailing for a resting spot, a sighting to say yes to. Time is now often seen as prolonged, without directional force, and—as for the Romantics—experiential rather than linear. Space, too, becomes indefinite, boundless. There is no other with which to locate the self; the poems are often literally caught in the self. The poems move into the realm of the harsh difficulty of discovery and include the possibility that the heart will not make any discovery at all.[46] There is here much less of the sense of the contained poem, the contained resolution, the sighting of the larger end.

Time and directional force have become so dissipated at the end of "No worst, there is none" that the speaker finds only a place to retreat to, where the chaos of the self need not be fronted:

> No worst, there is none. Pitched past pitch of grief,
> More pangs will, schooled at forepangs, wilder wring.
> Comforter, where, where is your comforting?
> Mary, mother of us, where is your relief?
> My cries heave, herds-long; huddle in a main, a chief-
> woe, world-sorrow; on an age-old anvil wince and sing—
> Then lull, then leave off. Fury had shrieked 'No ling-
> ering! Let me be fell: force I must be brief'.
> O the mind, mind has mountains; cliffs of fall
> Frightful, sheer, no-man-fathomed. Hold them cheap
> May who ne'er hung there. Nor does long our small
> Durance deal with that steep or deep. Here! creep,
> Wretch, under a comfort serves in a whirlwind: all
> Life death does end and each day dies with sleep.

The speaker is engulfed in the circular velocities of time without directional impetus, a spinning momentum that sucks him deeper into the vacancies of self where there is no exchange with the world, no gesture outward or assent.[47] The whirlwind is both the image and metaphor for the threatening circularity, momentum without direction, the dense solipsisms of the self detached from the world. The poem, with its unanswered questions and wildness of diction, is itself a chaotic whirlwind, a world without sign of linear redemptive time. The imagery of plunging into the unfathomed depths is another motion without will, control, or purpose—the infinite fall of Satan rather than the finite time of salvation. The poem enacts its propositions as it says them.

At the poem's close, the speaker makes a resolving proposition but not a redemptive one. He tells himself to himself to creep out of the whirlwind, to find respite from the chaotic momentum. Cessation of motion seems the best that can be hoped for. The last eleven monosyllables are hard and deliberate language, slowing momentum with thudding stresses: "all / Life death does end and each day dies with sleep." The speaker, weary beyond thought, seems to be dredging up the words one by one by a sheer effort of will. Each word is asserted in its time and sequence as if the speaker is consciously trying to reassert sequentiality and thus forcibly regain determinate time. The thought tries against odds to regain a sense of linear, finite experience by locating an end to the chaos.

Tormented and helpless, the speaker in this poem has lost his sense of a self that can reach out to the world, lost all trace of the first person subject, in the consuming experience of uncontrollable pain.[48] (Only Fury has an "I.") At the end, the poem seems to turn its back on the thought of assent, a thought now unendurable because the speaker can find nothing to assent to. It is a measure of his helplessness that the only gesture he can wish himself is retreat. He wants to withdraw and hide himself from sight, feeling, and most of all, consciousness.

In most poems, though, assent is possible and encouraged. The rising of self to meet and greet the external world yet remains differentiated response and not the univocality called for by the Romantic 'I am' of creation. And as the poet is to the world, the reader is to the poem—the subject-object distinctions are maintained. In Wordsworth, the poetry can approach much more closely to being the reader's unmediated response; in Hopkins, the speaker means to remain the object of the reader's perception. The reader's differentiated response to the poem is called forth by a poetic that insists on its own unmatchable *haecceitas*. For the reader, the process must remain a willed rising to meet, a striving toward, and not a dissolution into. In both writer and reader, the process is a time- and self-bound happening that preserves the reader's consciousness of the other, the speaker behind the voice.

And the reader is all the more sharply conscious of worldly time, of response, and of the confined self because of the movement of the poetry always yonder, always striving to reach a thing, a static place, that is not itself, that is beyond itself. Hopkins' unreachable ideal is one that denies the Wordsworthian process of a journey of gradual change or approach and is instead an act of heroism in man that spells total transformation and not merely assent—an apocalyptic event that would escape any located time and place and wholly transform the self. The nun's cry and the possibility that that might have been such an event, a final and instantaneous ascent, grasp the priest's imagination as nothing else— yet even there is his own awful uncertainty of cognition.

For the rest, apocalypse must await the resurrection, the immortal diamond-hooding, while assent, the only way man can and may respond, is the best that is possible within an imperfect human nature. The speaker moves in assent to God in the world: His poem *is* an assent. The reader responds to that assent by assenting to the poet in the poem, by reacting to the language that holds the strongly directed motion of the consciousness of an other.

II

Lyricism and Design

The Hopkins poem records the activity of its speaker in a language inherently active with gestures of assent. The activity of assent also extends to the poem's larger processes. For Hopkins, the directional turns of mind that occur in the poems are turns that should occur in the human mind. In turning from motions of densely figured sensual language, or lyricism, to motions of consciously chosen meaning, or design, the speaker shapes the poem's larger dynamics and makes an important assent. The turns of consciousness and language are not, as in the Romantics, subtle and progressive changes, but abrupt leaps, occurring quickly and with sharp definition. Much of the poetry's drama emerges from the direction, severity, and speed of those motions of consciousness and language; much of the drama emerges from the placement of those turns, from where they occur—and where they do not.

There is a recognizable pattern to the speaker's motions of consciousness in the Hopkins poem: The speaker leaps back and forth between witnessing the world and interpretation of it. His sharp, angular leaps shape the poem's dynamics and lend excitement and energy to the work. Although Hopkins is most often identified with his voice of excited, lyric exuberance, the voice that imposes argument or design on the lyricism, and so more consciously directs the lyricism to its ordained end, is essential to his vision.

The speaker insists on directing the lyricism, insists on the (highly un-Romantic) formulation of didactic meaning out of experience. The formulation, which often seems to involve an effort of conscious will, reveals something of the difficulty with which it was won by the extent of its leap of both consciousness and language.

The voice of lyric exuberance is more readily recognizable than the voice of design, perhaps because it is more elemental, summoning from physical, not rational, entities the cause of poetic activity. Still, though lyric exuberance about the world may be elemental, Hopkins' language of lyricism is complex indeed.

The world space to which Hopkins responds most readily is filled space, space crowded with sensory impression. Hopkins meets such space with eagerness, and the poems too are crowded, filled, brimming. Within a relatively small canon and within poems that only rarely run to more than twenty lines or so, the poet repeatedly impresses the reader with the feeling of inexhaustible energy. For the reader, this is known territory—a recurring and seemingly unstoppable pouring forth, an abundance of images, names, sounds, actions, things.[1]

Perhaps it is within the nature of lists to be infinitely expandable; at any rate, Hopkins' clusters or catalogues of images push, press outward and onward, progressively swelling as they take on momentum. The poetry seems to take joy in its own language, delight in its own fertility. The language is excited and exciting, active, and seems itself to participate in controlling the motion of the poem.

The reader soon grows sensible of language as a propelling force:

> Nothing is so beautiful as Spring—
> When weeds, in wheels, shoot long and lovely and lush; 2
> Thrush's eggs look little low heavens, and thrush
> Through the echoing timber does so rinse and wring 4
> The ear, it strikes like lightnings to hear him sing;
> The glassy peartree leaves and blooms, they brush 6
> The descending blue; that blue is all in a rush
> With richness; the racing lambs too have fair their fling. 8
>
> ("Spring")

The lines, like many others in Hopkins, thrust upon us a conscious awareness of language and sound. As the imagery begins, in line two, the word "weeds" seems to find the word "wheels" of its own volition—that is, we are probably aware of the similarity of sound between the two stressed words long before we have made mental or visual sense of the phrase.[2] In that same line, the process is repeated to a lesser degree when "long" seems to discover its followers, "lovely" and "lush." Perhaps that found word "wheels" brings us to the tiny blue thrush eggs, so complete and perfect that they suggest the whole firmament above; but the more obvious and forceful pull between the two images is the striking internal rhyme of "lush" with "thrush's." Again, the sound seems to be carrying us forward from one line to the next. Then, those still (and still to break open) "thrush's eggs" yield to the "thrush" itself, high above, his song in the heavens echoing through the echoing timber. Again, in their alliteration, consonance, and startling diction, the words "rinse" and "wring" (also heard as 'ring') insist that we know them as sounds first and only afterward as representations of actions.

What seems a new start in line six quickly regains lyrical momentum. The "echoing timber" has been singled into a "glassy peartree," which "leaves and blooms," but then those verbs of action are suddenly nouns, things, in the pronoun "they" which follows. The words, changing syntactical function, are active, moving. "They" has its own further action as the leaves and blooms color and touch ("brush") the "descending blue," the sky itself coming down to join in the joy and meet the world. Then "blue," the direct object, is repeated, now as a subject, where it is "all in a rush / With richness"—a fair description of the language itself.

In other words, before the speaker calls a halt at the end of the octave of "Spring," he shows us the dazzling vitality of the world coming awake—but also conveys the dynamic force of language and sound, and their power to influence and direct consciousness. In "The Windhover," "Spelt from Sibyl's Leaves," and "That Nature is a Heraclitean Fire," it seems as if the heady accumulation of the language of sense perceptions is willing the verse line beyond its conventional length.

Hopkins' lyric exuberance of language most often records nature, as in the early poems "Spring," "Hurrahing in Harvest," "The Windhover," and "The Starlight Night." But his lyric exuberance, his self-delighted language, extends itself to describe other things too: the physicality of man in "Harry Ploughman," the contours of a mind in despair in "Carrion Comfort" and "No worst, there is none," or the world running headlong to its own end in "Spelt from Sibyl's Leaves." The self-engendering impetus of language works to many an effect—including an apprehension that swells into horror when, in "Spelt from Sibyl's Leaves," what is best left unsaid will not stop saying itself.

In contrast, "Harry Ploughman" finds no reason to stop its delighted particularity of description:

> Hard as hurdle arms, with a broth of goldish flue
> Breathed round; the rack of ribs; the scooped flank; lank
> Rope-over thigh; knee-nave; and barrelled shank—
>   Héad and fóot, shoûldér and shánk—
> By a grey eye's heed steered well, one crew, fall to;
> Stånd at stress. Each limb's barrowy brawn, his thew
> That onewhere curded, onewhere sucked or sank—
>   Sõared ór sánk—,
> Though as a beechbole firm, finds his, as at a rollcall, rank
> And features, ín flesh, whát deed hé each must do—
>   His sinew-service where do.
>
> He leans to it, Harry bends, look. Back, elbow, and liquid
>   waîst
> In him, all quaîl to the wallowing o' the plough. 'S cheek
>   crimsons; curls
> Wag or crossbridle, in a wind lifted, windlaced—
>   See his wind- lilylocks -laced;
> Churlsgrace tọo, chíld of Amansstrength, how it hangs or
>   hurls
> Them—brõad ín bluff híde his frowning feet lashed! raced
> With, along them, cragiron under and cold furls—
>   With-a-fountain's shining-shot furls.[3]

The octave sees Harry at rest, the sestet pictures him in motion, and the poem exists in and for its powers of imaging the object of its attention. Hopkins may have been speaking to this when he wrote to Bridges, "The rhythm of the sonnet . . . is altogether for recital, not for perusal (as by nature verse should be)."[4] Perhaps the ploughman bending down to his "shining-shot furls" recalls the image of "The Windhover": "shéer plód makes plough down sillion / Shine." If so, the syntactically tortuous sestet which pictures Harry Ploughman in motion, leaning to his work, may well recall the windhover's buckling, the sacrifice, as the ploughman's Michaelangelan body yields itself to its appointed end. The wind lifts and laces through his "lilylocks" as he works, forming a halo in the speaker's eyes and figuring a natural ascent. Hard physical labor nearly always suggests a kind of holiness to Hopkins.[5] The final "shining-shot furls" surely refers at once both to the plough-man's locks and to the earth he works: a natural communion. Still, this is rather slight 'meaning' for a Hopkins poem and never really made explicit. Finally, the "emphatic recitation" that Hopkins calls for serves to lend stress, understanding, and drama to what remains a vivid picture; in fact, Hopkins calls the poem a "direct picture of a ploughman, without afterthought."[6]

"Harry Ploughman," then, exists for its implied assent to a stated and changing image, the poem's control coming with difficulty from its form and syntax. The rush of imagery makes no attempt to end but spreads out to be the whole poem, moving from the detail of tension and muscle in the ploughman's still body to the gathering and rushing of motion. Hopkins' elaborate metrical notations suggest that the poem may even have come about as a kind of technical challenge, testing how far a poem could go when its language was limited to description. Finally, the poem seems to turn back in upon itself. For all its hurling and lashing and lacing, there is a curious stillness to the whole— language serves to translate the eye's impressions and never much escapes the eye's constraints. The struggle centers wholly in the speaker's finding of language to say what he sees rather than in his finding of meaning.

Such naming of things, such lyricism, does assent to the world, but Hopkins is not often content with implicit assent alone. He does not often allow himself to dwell in such narrow confines of unformulated assent. Instead, he wants to clarify and confirm that assent by finding or reiterating the truth it illustrates. So in other poems, at some point the rush of imagistic language ends. The speaker calls a halt, often dramatically, by a keen change in direction. Notional assent confirms real assent, and so abstract statement, sometimes only posing as deduction, follows hard upon the rush of imagery. The effect is to wrest the poem back into its linear progress toward an end, back into time and design in time. The abstracting consciousness that discovers design is a familiar presence in Hopkins, for the language marked so strongly by its lyricism is the same language that Elisabeth Schneider rightly calls a "poetry of statement."[7] Hopkins' language seeks to convince its readers of important, general, and objectively stated truths. The presence of notional assent, God's design named, lends direction and purpose to the lyricism: "The world is charged with the grandeur of God"—and that, with all the force that the copulative holds in Hopkins.[8]

We focus, then, on the distinction between 'lyricism,' the sometimes overwhelming but always distinctive calling out of sense perceptions, of description, that is so marked in Hopkins' exuberance of language, and 'design,' those moments when order is imposed and the poem's process of cognitive reasoning is asserted and developed. The distinction between lyricism and design is admittedly bald—and often the two cannot be separated at all—yet the dichotomy arises plainly in a surprising number of Hopkins' poems. The sense of design is highly developed, stressed; outline and direction of argument are explicit. But so, too, is the sense of lyricism developed and stressed, and the poetry is perhaps more frequently identified with this quality. The two modes of development, forcibly set at odds, seem at times to be arguing the poem back and forth between themselves. The shift from one to the other is decisive, commanding attention and again stressing the speaker's willed activity of consciousness.

"Inversnaid," which describes a cascade of water near the town of Inversnaid, readily exhibits the dichotomy:

This darksome burn, horseback brown,
His rollrock highroad roaring down,
In coop and in comb the fleece of his foam
Flutes and low to the lake falls home.

A windpuff-bonnet of fáwn-fróth
Turns and twindles over the broth
Of a pool so pitchblack, féll-frówning,
It rounds and rounds Despair to drowning.

Degged with dew, dappled with dew
Are the groins of the braes that the brook treads through,
Wiry heathpacks, flitches of fern,
And the beadbonny ash that sits over the burn.

What would the world be, once bereft
Of wet and of wildness? Let them be left,
O let them be left, wildness and wet;
Long live the weeds and the wilderness yet.

Although the described scene in stanzas one through three is densely figured, the thought that the scene engenders in stanza four is not. The imagistic lyricism is sharply separate. The speaker sees the dark running of the mountain stream, here compared to a wild horse running, as it flows down into darkness and then emerges into light.[9] The darksomeness is seemingly redeemed when the stream falls to a whirling pool, pitchblack, which "rounds Despair to drowning." (Even in the earthbound and unconscious stream, it is vertical motion which is dramatically telling.) Having passed out over the pool's broth, the stream finds itself lightly running, banked on either side by a glistening, growing nature. In other words, the first three stanzas, replete with moving imagery, are primarily picture and give only the barest suggestion of meaning: In the water's dark and wild running downward and its subsequent emergence into light, a natural fall and rise of nature occurs—evidenced not only in the fresh dewiness and light of

the third stanza but also in the gaiety of the movement and trip-
ping rhythms.

Thus, the argument of the fourth stanza is not really anticipated:

> What would the world be, once bereft
> Of wet and of wildness? Let them be left,
> O let them be left, wildness and wet;
> Long live the weeds and the wilderness yet.

The syntax, diction, and rhythm are suddenly plain and highly
repetitive. The intensely specific imagery has yielded to a highly
generalized conclusion or prayer, a radical departure in language
from the densely textured first three stanzas. Geoffrey Hartman
has noted that Hopkins' poems

> do not seem to progress by thought to which word and
> image are subordinate, rather by word and image distill-
> ing thought. Where another poet might use statement,
> elaboration, suggestion, or grammatical emphasis, Hop-
> kins will use word on word, image on image.[10]

In "Inversnaid," it seems not so much that word and image have
distilled thought as that word and image have been pushed aside
to make room for the thought that must appear. The burden of
preparation for the poem's end rests in the implicit beauty of the
described scene and in the implicit value that beauty holds for the
speaker. The parallel, lightly running rhythms of stanza three do
provide some formal linkage when they begin to pattern the fecund
wilderness (of scene and language) into more regular sound. But
the turn toward meaning in the final stanza, the design born of
the lyricism, leaps all the way from one particular image of beauty
to the fear of an entire world without any. The speaker turns
away from the discrete image, in present and particular space, and
toward the question of its design in time.

That turn toward design in time does more than make meaning
clear. It relieves the stress of the here and now, providing a quieter
home apart from the physical energy and tension of the world. In
its repeated words and liquid sounds, in its hypnotic rhythms,

the concluding stanza suggests the sounds of prayer. Conflict still exists in the imagined possibility of a world without wilderness, but it is conflict of another order. In its redirection, the last stanza removes itself from the tensions of the immediate scene and the language necessary to describe it.

In Hopkins, the struggle against a too-engrossing lyricism is marked. Again and again, the assent to and of sensuous description, close and emotional, is reined in and controlled with an all-embracing generalization. The generalization or abstraction, the naming of the larger design, uncovers the underlying coherence of the energies of the disparate motions depicted. With reluctance or relief, the speaker pushes his attention into another direction, determined to find out what the perceived motions mean. And the two modes tell, "each off the óther." At the end of "Inversnaid," only the speaker's earnestness and the turn enacted provide the stress that would balance the complexity of the earlier stanzas. If justification for the last stanza exists, it is earned precisely through the previous effort of language.

In a few of the poems most obviously divided, the demands of the Italian sonnet form are thus answered, the sestet marking the point where the speaker explains where the word rush all 'goes.' In "Spring," after the initial, exuberant description, the speaker steps back at line nine to question, "What is all this juice and all this joy?" That is, he asks *about* the natural phenomena he has witnessed and named; the question is once removed from the sensuous apprehension of nature. Furthermore, the question specifically directs the rest of the poem. The speaker must now answer himself, explaining whence came the juice and the joy and what their end is. Similarly, in "The Sea and the Skylark," the sestet is used to comment upon the two phenomena in relation to man, bringing the early descriptions home: Man, who ought to be better than either sea or skylark, has lost both cheer and charm and continues to degenerate.

The motion toward design is a motion toward a more human going, cognition. Experience is re-vised, or re-seen, again and again, each act of revision reaching deeper into the world beyond the particulars physically seen. And the re-vision of vision attests to the continuing search for the original, absolute, and primal

design, *Ipse*. So the motion of consciousness toward design attests
to man's ordained purpose in the world.

If there is a single impulse to the direction in which Hopkins
searches out design, a single question that facilitates the finding,
it is 'Why?' In "Carrion Comfort," for example, Hopkins seeks
out the reason for the trial he has endured, and 'Why?' is the
understood antecedent to all his questions:

> But ah, but O thou terrible, why wouldst thou rude on me
> Thy wring-world right foot rock? lay a lionlimb against
>   me? scan
> With darksome devouring eyes my bruisèd bones? and fan,
> O in turns of tempest, me heaped there; me frantic to
>   avoid thee and flee?
>
> Why? . . .

It is 'Why?' the speaker asks about man's instinctive admiration of
the soldier: "Whý do we áll, seeing of a soldier, bless him?" ("The
Soldier"). It is 'Why?' he asks of a God who has seemingly with-
drawn his grace: "why must / Disappointment all I endeavour
end?" ("Thou art indeed just, Lord"). It is 'Why?' asked of religious
custom that directs "The May Magnificat": "May is Mary's month,
and I / Muse at that and wonder why"; "Why fasten that upon
her, / With a feasting in her honour?" In short, it is the 'why' of
experience that most seeks to be satisfied, for the something given
of experience, even in its plenitude, is not enough. For Hopkins,
the coming of the answer often is or implies quite another kind of
grace: "For I greet him the days I meet him, and bless when I
understand" (*Deutschland*, 5).

Typically, then, Hopkins satisfies his search for revision by dis-
covering the anterior design. He reaches to what is behind and
before the immediately perceived phenomenon. The speaker in
"Spring" moves back in time to find the origin, the "Eden gar-
den," that explains the "juice and joy" of here and now. Before
Margaret's weeping is the blight man was born for ("Spring and

Fall"); before the music's beauty is the composer's selving of self ("Henry Purcell"); behind the wreck of the Deutschland is the all-knowing will of God, whose vision can see so infinitely far in all directions that he knows the seeming cruelty of his might to be merciful.

"God's Grandeur" takes God's worldly design as its subject:

The world is charged with the grandeur of God.
    It will flame out, like shining from shook foil;   2
    It gathers to a greatness, like the ooze of oil
Crushed. Why do men then now not reck his rod?   4
Generations have trod, have trod, have trod;
    And all is seared with trade; bleared, smeared with toil; 6
    And wears man's smudge and shares man's smell:
        the soil
Is bare now, nor can foot feel, being shod.   8

And for all this, nature is never spent;
    There lives the dearest freshness deep down things;   10
And though the last lights off the black West went
    Oh, morning, at the brown brink eastward, springs—   12
Because the Holy Ghost over the bent
    World broods with warm breast and with ah! bright
        wings.   14

In antagonism to God's design, man's self-bent spoils the earth. Mimetically, the words in line six through seven seek to smear into one another, reflecting man's careless squandering of earth. But the sonnet gladly turns from this bleak vision of man's response to nature. "And for all this, nature is never spent": There is yet re-vision left, God's larger and grander design. "Nature is never spent" *because* "There lives the dearest freshness deep down things." Deep within nature dwells the inexhaustible source of newness, life. The second line at once illustrates, affirms, and explains the first.

Yet Hopkins is still not done. The final re-vision deals forth the further understanding, reason for reason, the 'because' of the 'because': "Because the Holy Ghost over the bent / World broods with warm breast and with ah! bright wings." Having penetrated far into the world ("deep down things"), the speaker's vision moves to the overriding, overwhelming cause of all that nevertheless springs from within. (The preposition is deliberate: The Holy Ghost broods "over," cares for, the world but is also physically positioned "over" the world as opposed to that freshness "deep down things.") The final revision is itself a promise of more, for it suggests the larger covenant intimated in the dawn. The world's morning dawns anew on and in the speaker's words, "and with ah! bright wings," a motion of language that fuses lyricism and design.

The turning to find the revision, the turning from the world's flux to its meaning in God's plan, is a conscious turning, a conscious search for the 'answer' which would dignify and still the original vision into a manifestation of enduring principle. In another sense, though, even the poetry's lyricism quiets the world.[11] The poet's sighting of the world's stress must still its tension; the stress beheld is further stilled in the poem, a fixed pattern on a finished page. The poet's apprehension stills the turning, catching the morning's minion, pinning it down in mind and language. Of course, this is true of any written account of experience, but in Hopkins one repeatedly feels its force. By lyricism and design, by image and didactic statement, Hopkins' speaker is always saying, '*Now* I have it. *This* is what it is.'

Still, although written language is necessarily a holder, a fixer, spoken language or speech partakes more of the motions that design impels. In a lyricism that demands to be heard, Hopkins strives for a motion of speech that could flow uncaught. He strives for a motion that would bid the reader to a more strenuous activity of knowing—in the words of the *Deutschland*, a "midriff astrain with leaning of, laced with fire of stress" (2). And this would be the transformation: to be able to be within the design, within the stress of lyricism, flowing with it, rather than standing over it, perceiving and imposing upon and revising it. It would be to *be* the 'yes' instead of to say it. It would be at last to be the pure stress of the nun's cry " 'O Christ, Christ, come quickly' " (*Deutschland*, 24) instead of the 'failed' apprehenders of it that the speaker and readers are.

The pure stress is apocalyptic, ultimately desirable, but other than human. Both the speaker and the reader are necessarily outside of pure stress, the unpremeditated and unselfconscious flight, and they both hold, behold, the tension—the "blue-bleak embers" that "Fall, gall themselves, and gash gold-vermilion." Cognition, awareness of design, proves worldly compensation for the consciousness which denies us apocalypse, our presence always rising toward and our failure always falling away from stress.

The Hopkins poem seems to know all this: As the lyricism strives for 'free fall'—strives in its speed, strangeness, and complexity to flow uncaught by the speaker's reflexive consciousness or the reader's beholding—the cognitive parts firmly impose design and dictate the resting places. In sharp contrast to the lyrical, detailed rush of world imagery in all its motion, come the authoritative generalizations. Often posed as superlatives, these absolutes and universals will even begin poems, seeming to anchor the images which follow in the certitude of cognition:

> Nothing is so beautiful as Spring—
>
> ("Spring")

> The world is charged with the grandeur of God.
>
> ("God's Grandeur")

> Glory be to God for dappled things—
>
> ("Pied Beauty")

> No worst, there is none.
>
> ("No worst, there is none")

These self-contained statements mandate a momentary stability while they distill the lyricism to follow. They ordain the subsequent rhyming and proclaim and assent to the design found.

Still, for all their decisiveness, abstraction, and stability, such statements are but readiers, holding the reader and the poem back in anticipation. To the practiced Hopkins reader, they are thematic setups, pressurized springboards before the plunge. Moreover, they again divide speaker from reader, for it seems likely that the poet's most recent process has been to infold or rhyme sense impressions into design, has been, in effect, an inductive process. The reader, who apprehends pattern before parts, who is prepared and groomed for the lyricism, undergoes a process more like deduction, for he proceeds from a pre-ordained generalizing principle. These patterns suggest that logic and design control the poem. But although the poem is shaped by design and offers dogma at the outset, the reader's experience of the poem centers in the accumulated empirical evidence gathered from the world, the lyricism that the poem then proclaims a manifestation of the absolute.

Lyricism and design, then, function in the poems both as modes of consciousness or ways of knowing, each gesturing its assent to what the other has said, and as recognizable poetic voices. Particularly in the short, early poems, where the voices seem most distinct from one another, design typically emerges in a language of extreme clarity, easily accessible to the reader. The clarity is fitting because Hopkins starts from a premise that the world's design is intelligible. The clear language of design is the more striking for being juxtaposed to the complex language and syntax that characterize Hopkins' lyrical voice.

Yet the two voices are not always so far apart in their language or difficulty of apprehension. Some poems are less boldly divided between the two modes, and the voices themselves often merge into a decidedly lyrical saying of design. So, while the problem of intelligibility in Hopkins centers in the voice of lyricism, it is not confined to that voice.

Intelligibility was important to Hopkins, who was adamant not only on the need to explain things but on the efficacy of explanation. "Explanation—except personal—is always pure good," he writes to Bridges:

> We should explain things, plainly state them, clear them
> up, explain them; explanation—except personal—is always pure good; without explanation people go on misunderstanding; being once explained they thenceforward

understand things; therefore always explain: but I have the passion for explanation and you have not.[12]

The "passion for explanation" recognizes and respects Hopkins' impulse toward truth saying. Explanation, often on a rather large scale, is a primary thrust of all his writing.

Moreover, his religious calling and his belief in the reciprocity of experience support not only his need to understand what he encounters but also a need to be understood. Explicitly or implicitly, Bridges must frequently have been urging Hopkins into plainer language, and Hopkins, within certain limits, accepted Bridges' response seriously, as something to be attended to. "However this new thing will be intelligible," he promises once; and later, more impatiently, he comments on "St. Alphonsus Rodriguez": "The sonnet (I say it snorting) aims at being intelligible."[13]

For of course both Bridges and Dixon found the going hard in reading Hopkins' poetry; Hopkins meets their bewilderment and misunderstanding time and time again. It must have been frustrating for a poet who was striving in so many ways for clarity and concreteness:

> I laughed outright and often, but very sardonically, to think you and the Canon could not construe my last sonnet; that he had to write to you for a crib. It is plain I must go no farther on this road: if you and he cannot understand me who will? Yet, declaimed, the strange constructions would be dramatic and effective. Must I interpret it? It means then that . . . . (O, once explained, how clear it all is!)

And once, weary and dispirited, trying to be resigned, Hopkins follows a long explanation of a misunderstanding with this comment:

> And indeed how many many times must you have misunderstood me not in my sonnets only but in moral, social, personal matters! It must be so, I see now. But

> it would embitter life if we knew of the misunderstand-
> ings put upon us; it would mine at least.[14]

In that last clause, he retreats into an admission of onerous, in-
escapable difference, his feeling of alienation from so much of
the life around him. That the poet who put so much energy into
meeting the world should feel so alienated is ironic; but Hopkins
is also the poet who knows that every being is unique and finally
locked within itself. Like the speaker of "No worst, there is none,"
Hopkins in this letter professes himself grateful for ignorance.

Still, such moments of despondency are relatively rare. Far more
often, Hopkins is energetically reaching out for experience and
what it may reveal and striving to make himself understood. If
to seem the stranger sometimes lay his lot, he pushes back hard
against that lot, and "the passion for explanation" is an essential
tool. Once, he proposes to write glosses, prose arguments for his
poems.[15] ("Henry Purcell" retains such a headnote.) Surely, too, the
diacritical marks that Hopkins devised for the poems are in large
part an attempt to make his meaning clear. Hopkins regretted the
need for such notation and was uncertain about whether to use it
or not:

> But which is the line you do not understand? I do myself
> think, I may say, that it would be an immense advance
> in notation (so to call it) in writing as the record of
> speech, to distinguish the subject, verb, object, and in
> general to express the construction to the eye; as is done
> already partly in punctuation by everybody, partly in
> capitals by the Germans, more fully in accentuation by
> the Hebrews. And I daresay it will come. But it would,
> I think, not do for me: it seems a confession of unintel-
> ligibility. And yet I don't know. At all events there is a
> difference. My meaning surely *ought* to appear of itself.[16]

Ideally, then, the poem makes itself known, and from this point of
view the notations seem "a confession of unintelligibility"; but
practically, a system of notation that would help make the poem
understandable attracts him. Hopkins' ambivalence is equally ap-
parent in another response to Bridges: "You were right to leave

out the marks: they were not consistent for one thing and are always offensive. Still, there must be some."[17] In fact, as Hopkins himself suggests, the diacritical marks—the stress, slur, pause, circumflex, and outride—ironically constitute another private language. In their attempt to further score an already dense poetry, they confront the reader with a visibly unfamiliar language. On the one hand, they want to make the reader hear and understand exactly what the poet said and meant: They want to clarify and explain. On the other hand, they set up another obstacle, another departure from the known, for the reader to master.

Hopkins' need to understand and be understood is more than every poet's need to be readable. Rather, it proceeds from very basic theological premises: that the world is intelligible, that man can within certain limits read its meaning, and that therefore man must do so. The turn from lyricism to design is an imperative, in the poem as in life. For Hopkins, the idea has as much reality as the thing—and considerably more stability. "My aim," Hopkins writes to Dixon of his poetry, "is to get the exact truth, & give that, with whatever colour."[18] This goal is not presumptuous (or impossible, as the Romantics would have it) but factual: The exact truth—of the world's image *and* argument—is there to apprehend.

The world is "word, expression, news of God"[19]—as "Pied Beauty" would make plain:

> Glory be to God for dappled things—
>   For skies of couple-colour as a brinded cow;
>   For rose-moles all in stipple upon trout that swim;
> Fresh-firecoal chestnut-falls; finches' wings;
>   Landscape plotted and pieced—fold, fallow, and plough;
>   And áll trádes, their gear and tackle and trim.
> All things counter, original, spare, strange;
>   Whatever is fickle, freckled (who knows how?)
>   With swift, slow; sweet, sour; adazzle, dim;
> He fathers-forth whose beauty is past change:
>   Praise him.

Only in retrospect does the reader see that the poem's first line ordains the whole. The abstracting design here holds, enfolds, envelops, the lyricism, while the discrete images held are examples and embodiments of the stable design that frames them. ('Glory be to God for these things. For these things, he creates: Praise him.') As the images mandate our understanding of their creation, our understanding of their creation mandates our praise of their creator. Whatever the difficulties of comprehending the lyricism, the voice of design in "Pied Beauty" is as clear and clearly stated as it is in "Inversnaid."

In contrast to "Pied Beauty," "As kingfishers catch fire" positions its clearest language of design at the poem's center. After four lines lyrically analogizing the world's phenomena, Hopkins turns to the argument, the thought distilled. After the densely patterned sounds and syntax of the first quatrain, these lines are relatively plain in diction, syntactical order, and density. "Each mortal thing does one thing and the same," the speaker explains, and then goes on to name what it is each does: It "Selves—goes itself; *myself* it speaks and spells." The contrast of language between these lines and the earlier quatrain is so marked that the poem implicitly suggests that, no matter how wonderfully complex and varied the world's phenomena are, the underlying truths are plain, accessible, and believable. That is, the relative simplicity of the language of design again lends it the force of truth.

In the poem's sestet, Hopkins extends the argument and the lyrical analogies to man:

> Í say more: the just man justices;
>   Keeps gráce: thát keeps all his goings graces;
> Acts in God's eye what in God's eye he is—
>   Chríst. For Christ plays in ten thousand places,
> Lovely in limbs, and lovely in eyes not his
>   To the Father through the features of men's faces.

By insisting that we acknowledge a speaker who is actually speaking ("Í say more"), Hopkins suggests an analogy with the stones, the tucked strings, and the bell's bow, objects named in the first quatrain, because each of these things selved, revealed themselves through sound. Since language, man's primary sound, is consciously determined, it is capable of deception and waste in ways that the other sounds mentioned are not, yet man *"can mean to give him glory."*[20] "Í say more" marks its own determination to do just that, stepping forward self-consciously to name its intention, reminding us that the speaker is dealing himself out in language.

The final tercet of the poem succeeds in piercing through the exciting but superficial beauty of the world to find the greater indwelling essence. The speaker reaches through superficial appearance for the deepest of causes only to find the inner principle shining outward and upward. Not as densely woven as the language of the first quatrain, not as insistently set out as the ordered, balanced syntax of the second, the last three lines fuse a beautifully relaxed lyricism with the final discovery of design, the innermost explanation: Christ's light reaching outward through man.

When that fusion of lyricism and design is achieved at the poem's end, it is as if Hopkins were discovering both principles in the world at once. The effect of the poem's end in "God's Grandeur," "As kingfishers catch fire," "Felix Randal," "Hurrahing in Harvest," and others is transcendent, the directed, reaching design that explains all emerging in a melting loveliness of language. But the fusion of the two voices poses some dangers too. The turn toward design is the sought-for revision of lyricism, but that turning is often hard-won. With his insistence on a poetry of cognitive explanation, Hopkins would not relinquish intelligible design; the fusion of voices must not obscure understanding.

"Henry Purcell" is earlier than "As kingfishers catch fire" but like that poem offers its plainest language of design and its clearest syntax in the second quatrain, near its center. In both sonnets, too, the final tercet seeks to explain through a lyrically said imagistic argument. But perhaps because Hopkins is here speaking about the problematic and interior artistic creation instead of the world creation, clarity of argument eludes the poem.

"Henry Purcell" examines what it is about Purcell's music that so impresses its hearer. It explores, then, artistic creation and response, and the mingling of inspiration with conscious, artistic intention. At the same time, the interplay of lyricism and design in the art object that is the poem comments subtly on what the poet says he is saying. The interplay of lyricism and design in the poem turns artistic inspiration into something necessarily 'unclear.'

In the second quatrain, the speaker defines the special element in Purcell's music first by naming what it is not and then by what it is:

Not mood in him nor meaning, proud fire or sacred fear,
Or love or pity or all that sweet notes not his might nursle:
It is the forgèd feature finds me; it is the rehearsal
Of own, of abrúpt sélf there so thrusts on, so throngs the ear.

This is relatively clear, directed argument, encased in a strong framework of definition. The lines exemplify the cognitive or intellectual faculty at work. But near the end, "Of own, of abrúpt sélf" and "so thrusts on, so throngs" are beginning to exert the lyrical pressure outward, beginning to 'break open' the poem at the center.

The sestet is still concerned with explaining what the music's specialness is, but the explanation now moves into a more intuitive, inspirational mode of knowing. Experiential and analogical, the sestet gives major image to both music and response:

Let him oh! with his air of angels then lift me, lay me!
    only I'll
Have an eye to the sakes of him, quaint moonmarks, to his
    pelted plumage under   10
Wings: so some great stormfowl, whenever he has walked his
    while

The thunder-purple seabeach plumèd purple-of-thunder,   12
If a wuthering of his palmy snow-pinions scatter a colossal
    smile
Off him, but meaning motion fans fresh our wits with wonder.

In the sestet, the compound structure of lines nine and ten reflects a duality of response to the music. The response begins with a mostly passive sensuality (Purcell's music is invited to "lift" him and "lay" him) but then adds a more active and willed cognition ("only I'll / Have an eye to the sakes of him"). As the first statement is qualified and turned around by "only," the second statement (lines eleven through fourteen) is qualified and turned by "but." The music's motion is like the stormfowl's; the speaker's dual response to the music, like his dual response to the stormfowl. The parallel syntax seems to gather up the bird's motion into a direct analogy to the music's motion. The stormfowl, "meaning motion," incidentally reveals the "forgèd feature" that elicits the observer's response. This is in fact the prose explanation which Hopkins rather drily offers to Bridges:

> The sonnet on Purcell means this: 1–4. I hope Purcell is not damned for being a Protestant, because I love his genius. 5–8. And that not so much for gifts he shares, even though it shd. be in higher measure, with other musicians as for his own individuality. 9–14. So that while he is aiming only at impressing me his hearer with the meaning in hand I am looking out meanwhile for his specific, his individual markings and mottlings, 'the sakes of him'. It is as when a bird thinking only of soaring spreads its wings: a beholder may happen then to have his attention drawn by the act to the plumage displayed.[21]

Hopkins' reading, then, posits "stormfowl" as the subject of "fans fresh" in the poem's last line. The stormfowl, "thinking only of soaring," "meaning motion," excites our wonder as the music of Purcell does. Natural inspiration, then, illustrates the nature of artistic inspiration.

Yet Hopkins also writes to Bridges that "the sestet of the Purcell sonnet is not so clearly worked out as I could wish,"[22] and the sestet's parallelism suggests another reading that would leave the stormfowl behind in the last verse. From this point of view, the verb after the colon is understood: "so [it happens when] some great stormfowl. . . ." In this reading, the sentence is compound; the second subject is "motion"; and intentional artistic creation contrasts with and is more wondrous than a natural act. So, "but meaning motion fans fresh our wits with wonder" returns the poem firmly to Purcell's uniqueness. Consciously composed to praise God, Purcell's music—and indeed Hopkins' poem—has meaning in a way that natural motion cannot.

Hopkins supports such differentiation of man and nature. Natural objects and beings

> tell of him, they give him glory, but they do not know they do, they do not know him, they never can. . . . This then is poor praise, faint reverence, slight service, dull glory. Nevertheless what they can *they always do.*
>
> But AMIDST THEM ALL IS MAN . . . man can know God, *can mean to give him glory.*[23]

The stormfowl is by nature more at one with the processes of inspiration than Purcell or Hopkins can be, and as if to confirm this, the stormfowl imagery is dense with the compound doubling of adjectives. Not so, the last verse. The last verse of the poem is a willful departure, pushing forward, insisting on poetic motion and argument come clear: "but meaning motion fans fresh our wits with wonder." The forged feature breaks out of and away from the unforged mass of language in the stormfowl analogy, and "meaning motion" becomes twice-over wonderful precisely because it is cognitive and consciously intends assent.

"Henry Purcell" draws on the Romantic rhetoric of inspiration. A correspondent breeze, something of the divine afflatus, is at work, with Purcell, the stormfowl, and the speaker each affected by it. "Let him oh! with his air of angels then lift me, lay me!" the speaker entreats, and his verbs look back to insist that "air" be taken literally as well as figuratively. Inevitably, the line recalls Shelley's "Ode to the West Wind." Only unlike Shelley, who wants to be rid of cognition, who prays to be lifted "as a wave, a leaf, a cloud!" and who goes so far as to regret the very poem he writes (because his ability to write means that he cannot *be* the wave, leaf, or cloud)—unlike Shelley, Hopkins immediately tempers his eagerness for that unthinking and unwilled sensual response to the wind. With determination he continues: "only I'll / Have an eye to the sakes of him. . . ." He posits an active and attentive response, a cognitive and willed finding of instress. Even so, at the close we learn that "meaning motion fans fresh our wits with wonder"; we learn that the attentive intellect ("our wits") is finally to be fanned or wakened *by* meaning motion—and into "wonder," a feeling that defies explanation. Finally, the process of response, active and passive, cognitive and sensual, is a cumulative inter-acting exchange that escapes all clear explanation.

The breeze informs all.[24] There is a "wuthering" of the fowl's wings (Hopkins defines the word as "the noise and rush of wind"[25]). Purcell's work also mingles intention with an uneasy holding of artistic inspiration: An "arch-especial . . . spirit . . . heaves in Henry Purcell." The wording suggests that the spirit is something contained with difficulty, something that shapes and moves Purcell but is not—at least not wholly—his.

The poet and his poem are like Purcell and his music, and both are like and unlike the stormfowl and his motion. For the poet, there has been a kind of conflatus, a coming together of Purcell's motion and the stormfowl's, to inspire the poem. The language of definition gives way to the lyrical impulse, and then, at the end, Hopkins consciously pushes that impulse aside. He forges a clarity of motion and language, a succinct and conscious explanation of event. That he does so insists on human cognition and intention. But ironically this very 'clarity' of language is in its own way as intangible, complex, and subtle as the inspiration it seeks to re-spond to and explain. And just once in the letters, Hopkins an-swers Bridges' desire for clarity with the understanding that some things cannot and *ought* not to be clear:

> Plainly if it is possible to express a sub[t]le and recondite thought on a subtle and recondite subject in a subtle and recondite way and with great felicity and perfection, in the end, something must be sacrificed, with so trying a task, in the process, and this may be the being at once, nay perhaps even the being without explanation at all, intelligible.[26]

The argument between design and lyricism in the poetry brings out a related and more encompassing tension in Hopkins' lan-guage, the argument between the mediatory and autonomous roles of language itself. It is a real conflict, the conflict between the procession of consciousness and the procession of language, because the poem needs both processions to exist. The poem needs to see itself as self-contained language and then to use that language to reveal a moving perception, a motion of consciousness that indicates the world.

When language in its autonomous role is restrained, the design of consciousness and world can be addressed. But when language goes too far in the direction of self-indexing—when the autonomous processional threatens to overwhelm consciousness and world, when language is no longer tracing the consciousness of event but is rather a sound without reference—when this happens, language ceases to serve anything outside of itself and ceases to fulfill any larger design. In fact, such language embarks on the destruction of all design, all intelligibility. Ultimately, it must become the language of no thing, of non-sense—and to be without sense is to be without direction, goal, and referential meaning.[27]

Admittedly, language-as-language-alone has considerable appeal. Relieved of all constraints, liberated from the world it had served, it is free to be Narcissus, to celebrate only itself, unburdened by meaning or design. As language seeks in its solipsism to escape its calling, seeks to envelop time and obliterate design, it seeks to become pure sound, and in pure sound is no tension at all. If language did succeed in this, it would consume the moment of its inception and its intention with it; absolute spontaneity, it would erase the traces of duration between thought and saying, the act of mind in its figuring of pattern. This is its peril: Completely autonomous language would not only be narcissistic; it would be dionysian, composed of an energy so dense that it would consume the energy of the poem, the speaker, the poem, and the design. Such language would abort all meaning and form in order to deify its own sensuality.

In Hopkins especially, this final, hellish pleasure must always be withdrawn; the tracing of consciousness must be firmly preserved; the conflict between the two languages in discourse must be preserved, for the poem's meanings—and meaningful energies—reside in the conflict between language as a self-contained master and language as a subservient tool.

In Hopkins especially, language must obey the call toward consciousness of the world because for it not to perform that charge is for the poet not to assent to and celebrate the real and meaningful creation—and poetry for Hopkins, as for any religious poet, must be ancillary and subordinate to that real creation. Man must *mean* to give glory. At the same time, the tension—between language essentially autonomous and language basically referential—sharpens because Hopkins is so drawn, particularly in his lyrical voice, to the dazzling beauty of sound. The tension is tautly strung, a discomfiting motif of a stressful activity.

For the reader, that stressful activity is known each time he finds himself given over to an awareness of and pleasure in complexly woven sound and language, reading unaware of meaning. The attraction of autonomous language is felt most in the voice of lyricism, when the language's sound seems to rise up and dominate the progress of the poem, when it seems to be in control of sense. In "Spring," in "Inversnaid," in "Pied Beauty," the restoration of clear design comes as a felt imposition, re-establishing cause and effect, reimposing order on sound, and consciously reaching back to gather the sound into the order. Yet the clear alternation of the voices is perhaps less dangerous than their merging; the tension of the stressful activity grows great indeed when lyricism and design subtly play within one another. Then the pull of the autonomous language may threaten to overwhelm sense, direction, and design.

The poem, then, must exist *between* the two polarities of language, the struggle held in check yet going on. The reciprocal flux reveals, charges, and discharges energy in its pulling away and pushing toward the sensual pleasure of language that exists in and for itself. This is a major source of drama in Hopkins, for poems are enactments of processes other than the processes they semantically name.

Ultimately, the drama enacts the presence of the language-sayer, the poet who is also a priest and the priest who is also a poet. "To what serves mortal beauty?" asks the speaker, and the question, with its assumption that human beauty must have a goal and be useful, is telling. Like nature, mortal beauty is a source of danger for man as well as an imaging forth of the creator. Man, the speaker concludes in this poem, must constrain the too blissful eating of forbidden fruit:

What do then? how meet beauty? [|] Merely meet it; own,
Home at heart, heaven's sweet gift; [|] then leave, let that alone.
Yea, wish that though, wish all, [|] God's better beauty, grace.

Assent ("Merely meet it; own . . . heaven's sweet gift") and design (the willed turning away, "then leave, let that alone") are the tools not so much discovered as named. Hopkins' thematic solution here—a brief enjoyment, a recognition of heavenly origin, and a willed abstinence—says much, reminding us again of the movement of poems wrenched away from the runaway lyricism into a firm recognition of design. Hopkins anticipates the struggle of Yeats and others against a too-ready lyricism, but Hopkins' struggle is at least as much moral as aesthetic.

The danger of the seductive mortal beauty of sound inheres in the very fabric of poetry.[28] In this context, as Howard W. Fulweiler's fine essay on Hopkins has shown, Hopkins' reading of the fall of angels is especially revealing.[29] As Hopkins tells that story, Lucifer ceases to serve, revere, and praise only when he is drawn aside and seduced by the beauty of his own (autonomous) voice in choir.[30] It is during a *song* to God that Lucifer's moral sense begins to waver as his attention wanders; he begins to hear his own voice to the exclusion of what it is saying, and so he begins to praise himself instead of God. It is like the lure of the Sirens calling Ulysses away from his designed goal, his journey home, but in Hopkins infinitely more dangerous because the sound that is swerving away from its goal is emerging from the self; the self is creating a sound without external direction, a sound that does nothing but proclaim the self. Hopkins' mandate for the proper response to human beauty was clear: "Merely meet it; own, / Home at heart, heaven's sweet gift; [|] then leave, let that alone." Lucifer prolongs the 'meeting,' allowing a glimpse of 'mortal' beauty to become all-consuming, and so refuses to acknowledge that the beauty is "heaven's sweet gift."

In short, in Hopkins' telling, Lucifer forgets the design; he di-

vorces the sound from its origin and goal. It is the beginning of
the end:

> This song of Lucifer's was a dwelling on his own beauty,
> an instressing of his own inscape, and like a performance
> on the organ and instrument of his own being; it was a
> sounding, as they say, of his own trumpet and a hymn
> in his own praise. Moreover it became an incantation:
> others were drawn in; it became a concert of voices, a
> concerting of selfpraise, an enchantment, a magic, by
> which they were dizzied, dazzled, and bewitched.

The "concerting of selfpraise" destroys the direction and thus the
assent:

> They would not listen to the note which summoned each
> to his own place (Jude 6.) and distributed them here and
> there in the liturgy of the sacrifice; they gathered rather
> closer and closer home under Lucifer's lead and drowned
> it, raising a countermusic and countertemple and altar,
> a counterpoint of dissonance and not of harmony.[31]

As Hopkins goes on, the angels convince themselves that what they
are doing is secretly pleasing to the lord, "divine and a meriting
and at last a grasp of the godhead."[32] (From Hopkins' religiously
committed point of view, the Romantic's deification of self, the
Romantic idea of the poet-priest, could hardly be better described.)
Having once turned away from their divine reference, their rever-
ence, the angels fall into the total dissonance of self-love. In the
mortal beauty of human sound, then, inheres the ultimate danger
of forgetting the ultimate design. In the pull of autonomous lan-
guage, associated most with the voice of lyricism, inheres the echo
of the first fall from grace and the temptation to reenact it.

"Spelt from Sibyl's Leaves" proclaims itself mediatory language
in its title. The title says that the prophecy that follows has been
"spelt"—decoded, read—and that the poem is therefore exegetical,
an interpretation of nature.[33] Yet the sibyl's meanings are notori-

ously unreadable, and in its struggle to express meaning, the poem does not discover the language of translation, the clear decoding of a sibyl's tale. Rather, perhaps more than anything else that Hopkins wrote, the poem becomes an event within itself wholly inseparable from the pull of its own articulation, its own self-pointing:[34]

> Earnest, earthless, equal, attuneable, | vaulty, voluminous,
> . . . stupendous
> Evening strains to be tíme's vást, | womb-of-all, home-of-all,
> hearse-of-all night.   2
> Her fond yellow hornlight wound to the west, | her wild
> hollow hoarlight hung to the height
> Waste; her earliest stars, earlstars, | stárs principal, overbend
> us,   4
> Fíre-féaturing heaven. For earth | her being has unbound; her
> dapple is at end, as-
> tray or aswarm, all throughther, in throngs; | self ín self
> steepèd and páshed—qúite   6
> Disremembering, dísmémbering | áll now. Heart, you round
> me right
> With: Óur évening is over us; óur night | whélms, whélms,
> ánd will end us.   8
> Only the beakleaved boughs dragonish | damask the tool-
> smooth bleak light; black,
> Ever so black on it. Óur tale, O óur oracle! | Lét life, wáned,
> ah lét life wind   10
> Off hér once skéined stained véined varíety | upon, áll on twó
> spools; párt, pen, páck
> Now her áll in twó flocks, twó folds—black, white; | right,
> wrong; reckon but, reck but, mind   12
> But thése two; wáre of a wórld where bút these | twó tell, each
> off the óther; of a rack
> Where, selfwrung, selfstrung, sheathe- and shelterless,
> | thóughts agaínst thoughts ín groans grínd.   14

"This sonnet," wrote Hopkins to Bridges, "shd. be almost sung,"[35] and indeed it is difficult to read without almost singing, so forceful and self-declaring are its sounds and rhythms. A cluster of images is no sooner over than the reading voice finds itself caught in a new web of sounds in the next cluster of words. The pause that is needed—that the thought, syntax, and voice seem to demand at the end of line three, for example—turns into no pause at all, the next word being stressed and an enjambment of the previous line. Then, in the next line the reader is caught within another series of sound- and stress-linked nouns in a series. The difficulty of the enjambment, the uncertainty of it, recurs between lines seven and eight, between lines eleven and twelve, and to a lesser degree, between six and seven, and ten and eleven. The poem's form derives from the sonnet, but even Hopkins was conscious of the extent of his departure: "I have at last completed but not quite finished the longest sonnet ever made. . . . It is in 8-foot lines and essays effects almost musical."[36] To add to the difficulty, the sonnet's rhythm is sprung, so the feet themselves are frequently far more than two syllables. The rhymes, sometimes slant, offer little sense of closure, and the lines are swollen far beyond iambic pentameter.

The speaker's impetus is the darkening of nightfall, the even-ing of powers of evening. As the pied world gradually loses its color and variation, its piedness, the gathering domination of black seems ominous in the extreme. In the light, the earth diffuses its dappledness, spreads and scales its this-ness; but drained, "her being has unbound." In a kind of cosmic entropy, the world drains back to an essential blackness beneath the stars. Past and future disappear, lost in the merging. Things fall together. In a sense, the speaker is Margaret matured, sensing his own end and *the* end, a universal fall back into an unconscious and undifferentiated, an unselved and static state of being, a womb-home-hearse.

The language is falling together too, the words collapsing in on themselves ("earliest stars, earlstars, ǀ stárs"; "all throughther"; "Disremembering, dísmémbering"). The rhythms of sense are falling rhythms ("womb-of-all, home-of-all, hearse-of-all"; "áll now"; "right / With"; as well as the strongly stressed, because strongly alliterated, adjectives in lists: "Earnest, earthless, equal"; "vaulty, voluminous").[37] Enjambment contributes to the sense of falling, with only three lines in fourteen coming to a full stop.

The first turn happens within the octave, an instinctual expression of fear fusing the self's reaction to the event, the reaction itself becoming the event upon which the poem will expand.[38] The speaker addresses his heart—a heart "right," as he points out, right in rounding him with the certainty of end that the night suggests. And it is the heart that speaks most plainly in the poem: "Óur évening is over us; óur night | whélms, whélms, ánd will end us." The poem—and the experience—center here, in the heart's seeing of the fearful and focal truth, the essential fact, the doom-of-all darkness. The directness of the 'over . . . whelming' end foreseen, the truth rounding the speaker, is bare and frightening.

Too frightening, perhaps, to dwell within it. For the speaker seeks escape, turns again to the conscious mental reading of the located scene. He resists the pure experience in an intellected explication, a language of mediation and mind, of explanation and proof: "Only the beakleaved boughs dragonish | damask the tool-smooth bleak light." But the piling up of forethought words does little to mask the simplicity of syntax, and the concentrated effort of mind begins to dissolve or diffuse in the simpler repetitive language that follows: "black, / Ever so black on it." The exclamation then leaps out of the effort of the struggle occurring. It is "Óur tale," "óur oracle," that the night enacts.[39] Within the darkness, the heart-truth in which the self enfolds itself—the unbound, unsheltered awareness of the final, 'pure' design—approaches unendurable knowledge, but no matter how little we want such knowledge, the blackness is ours. The prophecy is ours.

Although the imperative then seeks to push all of this away, to begin the priest's more formal 'teaching' in words directed at and to the world, the tone seems more and more self-directed. In hard irony, the words address a self that has not yet paid enough attention to this most essential 'before' and 'behind'—which is also essential after, over, under, and within. The speaker seems to chasten himself for not having *seen* before, using the stark words of description to dig the unwanted knowledge into the mind's eye.

The teaching attempts the clarity familiar from other poems as the speaker reaches to apprehend a world whose texture will have unraveled, one which has evenly parted, penned, and packed the

all into two irrevocable flocks—"black, white; ǀ right, wrong."
The metaphors, although they come fast, are threadbare, them-
selves unbound. The imperatives emerge harshly, repeating their
insistent demand that the self now, at last, look at, fix attention
upon, and properly fear the appointed end: "a wórld where bút
these ǀ twó tell." Diversity, all selfhood, is abolished in this picture
of a final, an ultimate intelligibility that ironically is no comfort
at all. The stark dualism is hellish, everything wound down and
packed into the yes and the no. At the last, after all the dapple, the
bare Christian dualism rises naked, stringent, and tormenting in
its absoluteness.

It is now, of course, at the end of the sonnet, that we expect
the 'why?' to be answered. "Wáre," the speaker has warned in his
harsh surety, "wáre" of this consuming dualistic design beneath
all; and taught by the sonnet's form, taught by Hopkins' own
persistence in discovering causation, taught too by his habit of
finishing a poem, we await the statement of God's plan come
clear. But contrary to all these expectations, the conclusion does
not come clear. The meaning residing within is not located. There
is no "To the Father through the features of men's faces," lyrical,
directed, transcendent. Nor is there "It is Margaret you mourn
for," the poignant explanation encased in strong closure. Here, in
"Spelt from Sibyl's Leaves," the self cannot reach the further ex-
perience that explains, nor even a distancing intellectual finality.
Instead, the bare description, for all its harsh fighting against the
experience, the event, falls back into the event it had sought to
explain. The parallel structure "wáre of a _____" seems in its
repetition a further clue that the language seeks the larger abstrac-
tion but, locked within the consequences of the experience of its
own imagery and language, cannot escape the more tormented
repetition: "of a rack / Where, selfwrung, selfstrung, sheathe- and
shelterless, ǀ thóughts agaínst thoughts ín groans grínd." The poem
refuses the ceremony of the poem, collapsing back into its own
event of pain. Given the choice of avoiding that event, even ob-
viously seeking to avoid it in its leading away from it, the poem
yet descends back into it, re-enters the realm of stronger experience
and re-enters it so strongly as to put the expected artifice, the

ceremony of the poem, to shame. As the harsh description becomes event, the poem denies us the comfort of known context and is itself overwhelmed by the inexpressible.

And yet the articulation of pain cannot be the event of pain— "Nor mouth had, no nor mind, expressed / What heart heard of, ghost guessed" ("Spring and Fall"). The poem finds itself trapped within its own being as a poem. Thus, the poem that refused to make ceremony still has its ceremony. Deritualized, it is ritualized anew. This is the crux of the poem's process, an irony of ironies as the poem relinquishes the idea of intelligible design in order to express the essential sound, the essentially inexpressible sound, and so ends after all in self-pointing meaning. "Selfwrung" and "selfstrung," the language cannot but call attention even more compellingly to itself. Having eschewed the reference outward, the reverence, the design, language erupts in a kind of self-reference, reverence, and design.

The rhythm alone would tell us this. In the last line, if, as would seem demanded, the adjectives of the first half line are each stressed, the "where"—although it is followed by a comma, although it is a homonym for the important "wáre" of line thirteen—cannot also bear stress. And in the next half line, we are directed to emphasize the words we would ordinarily not emphasize, to stress the prepositions and leave their ordinarily more important objects unstressed. The line is close to impossible to read, and Hopkins means the line to be awkward, the words to enact the grinding of groans. Yet it is by self-proclamation a dissonant self-pointing. It ends in intelligible delineation of unintelligible agony.

But this delineation is far different from the certitude that Hopkins achieves in other poems. All of his poems feel the pull of autonomous language, but through the clear restoration of design Hopkins reasserts mastery in a language disciplined and directed back toward its ultimate maker. We grow used to leaving the poems with a sure explanation of experience, a reaching behind and before to discover causation and end. More than any other poem in the canon, "Spelt from Sibyl's Leaves" is consumed by the event it had set out to bear witness to, and the poem thus tells its speaker's anguish by the distance at which it exists from Hopkins' usual patterns as well as by the burden of what it says. Elsewhere, Hopkins turns away from dwelling so exclusively in language and resolves to find and name the larger understanding of God's design in the world. That design implicitly blesses the poem, denying the hedonistic lyricism which exists solely for itself, arguing strongly for the world's intelligibility. The reader's experience is controlled and shaped by the poem's leaps of voice, by its alternating and merging currents of consciousness, as the language pulls toward and away from the extreme energy of the voice of lyricism.

III

Bidding

As the Romantic poem diminishes our awareness of the poem-as-created-artifact, drawing us into a more unselfconscious state of being with its apparent artlessness, it invites us to identify with and become the speaker whose words we read. Hopkins' poetry again stands in contrast. Although it also is filled with the apparently spontaneous, his is an exaggerated spontaneity; although it is filled with immediate reaction, its immediacy calls attention to itself and for itself, encouraging us to look at its response instead of becoming one with it. In short, Hopkins' speaker is so extreme in his activity of language, body, and consciousness that he frustrates the reader's falling away of self.

Gestures of assent and the argument between design and lyricism both help place the speaker at an extremity of self. These motions enact as well as say the right response to the world in sharp, recurring patterns which define the speaker's presence. What the speaker accomplishes with his dramatic motions of thought and his naming of action is apparent also in his rhetoric. Certain syntactical forms—the imperative, the exclamation, the interjection, and the question—reiterate and further our sense of his extreme activity. As syntax is again and again wrenched away from the calmer declarative statement, these syntactical forms dramatically activate the poetry's language. Like the motions examined in earlier chapters, the syntax Hopkins uses embodies right response to the world and so is yet another part of Hopkins' implicit grammar of assent, bidding us to similar action. At the same time, syntax again makes clear that the speaker is not the reader and that the reader must find such response for himself.

In 1882, Hopkins wrote to Bridges, commenting on the drama Bridges had written and sent him to read:

> I do not think it has in a high degree a nameless quality which is of the first importance both in oratory and drama: I sometimes call it *bidding*. I mean the art or virtue of saying everything right *to* or *at* the hearer, interesting him, holding him in the attitude of correspondent or addressed or at least concerned, making it everywhere an act of intercourse—and of discarding everything that does not bid, does not tell. I think one may gain much of this by practice.[1]

The idea is exact in terms of Hopkins' own poetry, in which the language bids, tells, speaks *"to* or *at"* its audience, expecting, asking, at times even demanding, response. Hopkins' poems are set up as colloquy between the speaker and God or world or self, yet they are reminiscent of drama and dramatic dialogue in their keen awareness of the audience, whose reaction seems an expected part of the drama. The poems often quite literally bid—plead for, ask, invite, exhort, or command—the reader to respond.

In fact, the rhetorical relationship that the poems embody is one of the poetry's strongest pulls upon us. The reader seems not to be 'overhearing' the speaker so much as he is being directly spoken to. The poems achieve this positioning by a variety of means, none of them really unusual to poetry, but in Hopkins accumulated to such a degree that their force is marked.

The poetry is, for example, filled with signs of an extreme spontaneity—all the coinings of words; the exuberant exclamations on the world; the breaking out from traditional, encrusted forms of meter and poem; and most of all, the speaker's continued attempt to break down the poem-as-poem in his overt beckoning to the reader to see what he sees: "Look at the stars! look, look up at the skies!" ("The Starlight Night"). At first glance, it seems as if the speaker has thrown away all the artifice, the convention that poetry is written language and not action in the world, as he spills over instead into a spontaneous excitement, an excitement that *means* to be contagious. Exhilaration, celebration, exclamation: These are all regular features of the poetry, features which make it difficult for a reader not to respond.[2] The very intensity of the speaker's emotion is compelling.

In *The Language of Gerard Manley Hopkins*, James Milroy argues persuasively that the uniqueness of Hopkins' language—of its diction and sounds, its rhythms and syntax—derives primarily from the spoken word; that when Hopkins wrote to Bridges that "the poetical language of an age shd. be the current language heightened," he was talking about the language currently being spoken, or speech.[3] Thus, while the speaker is reminding us of his physical selfhood by naming his bodily actions, his language reminds us of actual speech. Milroy's study suggests, then, an important reason why the Hopkins reader feels so called upon, even pulled, to react to the words and ideas before him. More dramatically and directly than in most poetry, Hopkins' speaker *is* a speaker.

The speaker who exclaims "Felix Randal the farrier, O is he dead then?" is vividly before us, responding personally and apparently spontaneously to the sudden news of the farrier's death. The words seem blurted out, unpremeditated, spoken in surprised dismay. Similarly, the opening of Hopkins' longest and most formal poem seems struck out of an actually speaking speaker on the moment: "Thou mastering me / God!"[4] At the outset of *The Wreck of the Deutschland*, the speaker is caught in a forceful and present-tense occurrence; his syntactical pattern tells us as much about the event as his words do. The more common poetic stance of a persona quietly reflecting or carefully telling a story is far distant. Since Hopkins moves in and out of such fragments of spontaneous exclamation often, and since, as Milroy has shown, the structures of speech inform all of Hopkins' poetry, the reader is the more likely to feel directly called upon by the poem.

Moreover, partly because of the influence of spoken language and because of the speaker's frequent spontaneous intensity, Hopkins' poetry has a way of encouraging us to trust in the speaker and in his sincerity. We may or may not believe the design the speaker names is objectively true, but powerful incentives convince us the poet strongly believes that what he says is true. The poet was, after all, a priest, and his religion and priesthood inform all of his work. Yet perhaps more important to the reader's trust is that even to the unpracticed Hopkins reader, the poetry forcefully impresses itself as the act of a single consciousness through time. Experimentation with subject, style, and voice, inevitable in any major poet, happens in Hopkins within relatively narrow confines. The mature Hopkins voice is singular, holistic, and unmistakable. We come to know and trust the speaker's seriousness and his sincerity in celebration or despair, just as we come to identify that speaker closely with the poet.[5]

In fact, Elisabeth Schneider has concluded that Hopkins "recognized no aesthetic or theoretical need for a separation between himself, Gerard Hopkins, and the speaker of the poem."[6] Hopkins noted, more than once, that his poems embodied autobiographical experiences.[7] Even putting the secondary sources aside, the poet's closeness to his speaker is readily felt. The intensity, consistency, and continuity of the work through time all make us want to merge the voice behind the poems with the "I" of the poems.

Moreover, Hopkins ignores many conventional poetic devices that create distance between the poet and his speaker. "As kingfishers catch fire" tells us that sound is action and that action, itself a language, spells being. As if to exemplify its own theses, the poem is filled with action and stressed sound:

> As kingfishers catch fire, dragonflies draw flame;
>   As tumbled over rim in roundy wells
>   Stones ring; like each tucked string tells, each hung bell's
> Bow swung finds tongue to fling out broad its name;
> Each mortal thing does one thing and the same:
>   Deals out that being indoors each one dwells;
>   Selves—goes itself; *myself* it speaks and spells,
> Crying *What I do is me: for that I came.*

Í say more:

Hopkins inserts the last words, "Í say more," into the poem's argument as if to remind us that there is a real speaker here, one who is actively doing (saying) something in the poem, dealing out himself. The forthright "Í say more" insists that the speaker is conscious of his speech, that he means what he says, and that he 'stands behind' his own words. Throughout Hopkins, we are encouraged to believe that the speaker is 'real,' a presence before us, just as all his namings of his own physical gestures would have him.

Yet no poet can ever completely be the speaker of his own poetry. At the same time that it is convincing us of its spontaneity and authenticity, Hopkins' poetry is forcefully bringing home George T. Wright's argument:

> However skillfully the poet may try to effect an identity between himself and his persona, the task is hopeless, for he and what he has created exist on different metaphysical levels. . . . The speaker is wholly a product, and only apparently a source.[8]

In Hopkins, the speaker is so extremely active and emotional, his language so often densely woven and dramatically active, that we soon realize we are facing the created object, and the highly crafted and disciplined language is only apparently spoken spontaneously.

The very pitch of activity, the singularity of the Hopkins poem, creates distances. In a brief introduction to the *Deutschland,* the contemporary poet and novelist James Dickey writes with enthusiasm:

> Hopkins is a poet of extremes, of the pushing of vision, the pushing of poetic devices beyond themselves, to a point one degree farther than the *reductio ad absurdum,* one degree higher than the ludicrous, which is in some cases the degree of sublimity. In no other poet, not even Shakespeare or Donne, is it quite so obvious to the un-warned reader that a new *dimension* has been added to poetry. All other poems, even some of those commonly called "great," are likely to seem linguistically thin, a

little prosaic and easily satisfied with themselves, compared with Hopkins. On first encountering Hopkins' intense, peculiar, rapid idiom, a great many people have said to themselves that here, at long last, is a *complete* poetry, working powerfully at all levels, at once both wild and swift beyond all other wildness and swiftness and stringently, savagely disciplined: a language *worked* for all it can give.[9]

Dickey's words are highly interesting in that they repeatedly reflect a truth about the reader's encounter with Hopkins' art: namely, that the reader is apt to sit back and admire the art, the 'working' of language, much more readily than in many other poets. The very "wildness and swiftness"—of the speaker *and* his language— may help put the reader at the slight remove wherein he objectifies the speaker and the poem, for the poetry quickly compels reaction to its craft.

That is, the poetry compels reaction to the representation as well as to what is represented. Emerson Marks aptly quotes Hopkins in arguing that our appreciation of any art object arises in part from our perception of what has been accomplished:

> We admire "the achieve of, the mastery of the thing," the manipulation of what seems especially precarious, difficult, ever threatening to get out of control. . . . aesthetic excellence, like moral, lies not in easy, one-sided conquest but in struggle long sustained and constantly in doubt.[10]

Marks speaks, as George T. Wright does, in the tradition of criticism stemming from Coleridge: The poet is involved in the dynamic reconciliation of opposites.[11] No one is more accessible to this line of criticism than Hopkins, whose words insist upon themselves as process, as struggle, as spontaneous bidding, and at the same time as product, as finished art object. It is not just that the poem exists as both; it is that the poem would be *known* as both. The extreme activity, then relaxation, the motions between design and lyricism and between autonomous and mediatory language, all make us as conscious of struggle as we are of form, discipline, and right outcome. "It is the forgèd feature finds me," Hopkins writes of Purcell's art. To forge anything is to work and work mightily; to work mightily is to proclaim the self. The "forgèd feature" proclaims its author at the same time that it exists as product, in and of itself. The "forgèd feature" bids our attention directly at the same time it is strongly asserting that it was crafted to that end.[12] The pronounced, highly dramatic patterns of consciousness, activity, and rhetoric of Hopkins' speaker are all such forged features.

For all its spontaneity and contagious excitement, then, the Hopkins poem refuses to subsume its reader as Romantic poetry does because the Hopkins poem is all the time making itself felt as an object to be admired. The abrupt turns, the unfamiliar diction, the highly dramatic syntax and rhythms insist on our consciousness of the poem-as-poem and so of ourselves as outside the poem. In so doing, the poem reasserts and reaffirms Hopkins' belief that there can be no ultimate sharing or merging of selves. For Hopkins, consciousness or feeling of self—what he called "self-taste"—"is more distinctive than the taste of ale or alum, more distinctive than the smell of walnutleaf or camphor, and is incommunicable by any means to another man."[13] Accordingly, his work proposes the inescapable *haecceitas* or 'thisness' of every being. So the poet as spectator is left outside the windhover, in wonder at its magnificent motion, and the nun's words defy his final comprehension. In fact, the closer he approaches, the more the impossibility of final oneness is felt.[14]

As the speaker is to the windhover, so are we to the speaker: stirred, moving out of ourselves in the response of assent, but finally closed out of oneness and ultimate knowledge, and perhaps left with heightened sense of self because of it. That is, the speaker's voice is so extreme in its emotion, its turns so abrupt, its speed so changeable, that we may end by being more aware of our own selves as distinct from the speaker. His naming of his own physical gestures, bold activity in the world, may also underscore our sense of his otherness. And the speaker's dramatically active language augments that sense rhetorically when it, too, demands differentiated response.

The imperative, the exclamation, the interjection, and the question repeatedly leap up from the more common poetic syntax of the declarative sentence.[15] These four structures, more typical of speech than of poetry or even written language in general, stress in Hopkins the speaker's spontaneity, his exuberance, and his 'authenticity.' They suggest that the poem is phenomenal activity. But the poem and its speaker also demand response on another level. Through the constraints of disciplined form, through the ways in which Hopkins uses those four structures, and through the very frequency with which they occur, the poem, in Hopkins' words, holds the reader "in the attitude of correspondent or addressed or at least concerned, making it everywhere an act of intercourse." The Hopkins poem demands, then, that the reader retain and more fully realize his own distinct selfhood.

The structure that most openly holds the reader in "the attitude of correspondent" is the imperative mood. The commands that Hopkins' speaker gives are sometimes quiet, sometimes strident, but whatever the tone of voice, the imperative lends a note of urgency to the words. And while the imperative mood implicitly bids the hearer into action, the frequently used and closely related metaphor of bidding gives explicit name and image to what the imperative does.

The excited, exclamatory imperatives of "The Starlight Night" insist that the moment be seized, that the world be seen sharply and at once, before it changes and is lost:

> Look at the stars! look, look up at the skies!
> O look at all the fire-folk sitting in the air!

Here, as in so much of Hopkins, the speaker's imperative is bent on rousing the hearer into action in the instantaneous present of the world.

Hopkins' imperative can also be quiet and firm. After an exuberant process of naming and categorizing the world, the conclusion of "Pied Beauty" comes in a still sureness.[16] The time is the present, but it is clearly the present of all time, the continuous present of God's presence in the world:

> He fathers-forth whose beauty is past change:
> Praise him.

The world's pied beauty is constant through time; beauty's imperative demand on man is equally so. In fact, the force of the poem's final line makes us recognize the poem's opening line—"Glory be to God for dappled things—"—as the imperative it is.

The use of the imperative in "Pied Beauty" suggests that Hopkins may have come to his reliance on the mood rather easily—the form is characteristic of hymns, prayers, and litanies. In fact, the speaker sometimes ends the poems with an imperative that, aimed at heaven, reaching up, functions as prayer. At the close of *The Wreck of the Deutschland,* the speaker hopes the nun who died will yet remember man by letting Christ "easter" in him. This prayer within prayer gently anticipates the appositive enclosuring that forms the poem's stunning last line:

> Dame, at our door
> Drowned, and among our shoals,
> Remember us in the roads, the heaven-haven of the
> reward:
> Our King back, Oh, upon English souls!
> Let him easter in us, be a dayspring to the dimness of us,
> be a crimson-cresseted east,
> More brightening her, rare-dear Britain, as his reign rolls,
> Pride, rose, prince, hero of us, high-priest,
> Our hearts' charity's hearth's fire, our thoughts' chivalry's
> throng's Lord.

In contrast, the conclusion of "The Blessed Virgin compared to the Air we Breathe" is far less ringing, far more intimate in tone, yet still controlled by the imperative prayer as the speaker figuratively looks up:

Be thou then, O thou dear
Mother, my atmosphere;
My happier world, wherein
To wend and meet no sin;
Above me, round me lie
Fronting my froward eye
With sweet and scarless sky;
Stir in my ears, speak there
Of God's love, O live air,
Of patience, penance, prayer:
Worldmothering air, air wild,
Wound with thee, in thee isled,
Fold home, fast fold thy child.

Here the tone is more familiar, the stanza a resting place that
gathers the poem into the desire for right conclusion that forms the
poem's conclusion. These imperatives are prayers for a future de-
fined by experience in and meditation on the past. Thus, Hopkins'
imperative, while it plants us firmly in present-tense speech, is
always pointing forward to a response that will fulfill the bidding.
Whether addressed to man or God, the imperative often sounds a
note of hope, of anticipation. At the very least, when the hope is
radically at odds with the situation the speaker sees, the imperative
voices a desire for change.

Hopkins' speaker even pleads with himself to change. The tradi-
tional 'public' prayer is internalized into a moment of sad tender-
ness and pity for his own troubled self:

Come you indoors, come home; your fading fire
Mend first and vital candle in close heart's vault:
("The Candle Indoors")

My own heart let me more have pity on; let
Me live to my sad self hereafter kind,
Charitable; not live this tormented mind
With this tormented mind tormenting yet.
. . . .

> Soul, self; come, poor Jackself, I do advise
> You, jaded, let be; call off thoughts awhile
> Elsewhere; leave comfort root-room; let joy size
>
> At God knows when to God knows what;
>   ("My own heart")

In both these poems, the imperative urges a stillness, a withdrawal from distracting variety, a close quietness. In effect, it here shapes prayers to the self. In "My own heart," the speaker, burdened by a harsh self-consciousness, repeatedly bids himself to turn away, to think of other things or not think at all, in order that there be the inner space that welcomes joy. The imperative calls him back from language that begins to swell with the naming of what is wrong; it redirects the self and the poem to better ends. Indeed, in "My own heart," the imperatives show that the change desired has been at least partly realized during the poem, for the second group of imperatives is far more resolute, more contained and controlled in syntax, than the earlier set.

In both "My own heart" and "The Candle Indoors," the speaker's extreme tenderness and even pity for himself make the reader feel the distraction, exertion, and worry to which the lines are responding. Thus, the imperative often implies a turning, for it most typically bids that something that is not so, be so. By its very nature, the imperative asks for change. The poetry is again *marked* by the excitement of turning, directional changes that make the extreme activity of consciousness known. With its implication of change (and its knowing so decisively what that change must be), the imperative is an essential part of the poetry's drama.

Between the imperative of strident command and the one of quiet tenderness is another tone of voice, a plea that gains force and earnestness through the use of the imperative. Here, the backdrop is the speaker's knowledge or fear that something may easily go wrong, and in response he urges right action in the world:

> What would the world be, once bereft
> Of wet and of wildness? Let them be left,

O let them be left, wildness and wet;
Long live the weeds and the wilderness yet.
("Inversnaid")

What do then? how meet beauty? | Merely meet it; own,
Home at heart, heaven's sweet gift; | then leave, let that alone.
Yea, wish that though, wish all, | God's better beauty, grace.
("To what serves Mortal Beauty?")

The lyrical incantatory bidding of "Inversnaid" and the imperative answer offered by "To what serves Mortal Beauty?" are both moral directives that emerge because the speaker knows that other, less adequate responses to beauty, a manifestation of God in the world, are possible and even likely. The imperative charge anticipates and fends off those less worthy responses, the destruction of beauty in the first poem, the deification of it in the second.

That man determines himself and controls his own actions is implicit in the imperative, as manifest in each example as the ethical responsibility that calls the imperative forth. "You there are master," the speaker of "The Candle Indoors" tells himself; "do your own desire." But the imperative structure, so much a part of Hopkins' voice, goes further, positing an interaction of language and deed. In its order to action or behavior, the imperative expects—or better, 'bids'—response. It assumes that words affect and effect, or at least that they are capable of doing so. Moreover, like so many of the techniques of Hopkins' poetry, the imperative is often a visible product of self-consciousness. It signals that the speaker has drawn back from the world or from a present course of action or thought in order to demand change—and it does this even when the change demanded amounts only to an intensification of what already is. Overtly self-conscious, the speaker treats himself as an 'other' and spurs himself on to right, and therefore significant, action. (It is worth noting how very many of the imperative commands involve verbs of motion—and how even the intransitive verbs acquire rhetorical force when put in the short, sharp form of the imperative verb.)

In 1885 in an untitled lecture on duty, Hopkins wrote of the "voice which conscience hears":

The thing it would bring about and bids is what we call
Right or moral good, the thing it would prevent and
forbids is Wrong or moral evil. . . . duty requires further
the notion of bindingness and law, . . . and this we recog-
nise in the stress put upon us by that voice of command
which directs us to do or forbear, which bids or for-
bids us.

When Hopkins fills his poetry with imperative bidding and for-
bidding in order to urge right action, he is dramatizing belief,
externalizing and making active an interior bidding through struc-
ture and motion of language; he is finding the form that acts out
what he wills the words to say.

The "voice which conscience hears" resembles in its phrasing
the spirit which "heaves in Henry Purcell." Both phrases suggest
something there for man to use but not to own, a gift. Hopkins'
imperative voice is that of God, and it is at least partly within us:

Therefore the voice which commands conscience is the
voice of God or it is God as a lawgiver commanding, and
so we have an immediate perception not of God's self
and essence indeed but of his will towards us.[17]

In this sense, the speaker is merely passing the imperative on to
his audience, for as both the prose and the poetry make clear, God
and his world do their own bidding: "But thou bidst, and just
thou art" ("Thee, God, I come from, to thee go"); " 'A crimson
East, that bids for rain' " ("The Nightingale"). In this sense a medi-
atory figure, Hopkins' speaker becomes the moral and sensory
teacher to the poem's audience, be it himself or another reader,
and responds to the bidding of the world's intelligibility and the
voice that conscience hears. The use of the imperative encourages
the human response that the world calls for; it bids for and would
direct attention and action but leaves the reacting will still free.

Moreover, through the speaker's ability constantly to see him-
self, to talk to and answer himself (as seen in the imperative), the
poetry grasps the *reader*, involving him in the give and take of
experience. It does so because the audience of the imperatives is

unnamed—the reference is ambiguous. Although it may take no clear-cut notice of the reader, although it may at first or at last be read as self-directed on the part of the speaker, the imperative is one of the poetry's strongest bids on the reader. "Come you indoors, come home; your fading fire / Mend first" explicitly uses the second person, while "leave, let that alone" merely implies the 'you'—but both assume direct communication with an audience. By making it momentarily seem that we are spoken to, the imperative takes the reader into direct account, mandating not only present consciousness but future action, outside the poem. For a moment, the poem overtly acknowledges the *reader* as the other and quite literally bids our response.

Always bidding the reader through the liberal use of the imperative, the poetry also openly images the idea of bidding through its metaphors. Hopkins figures nearly all relationships within the dynamics of a give and take. The energies expended in apprehending something other than self return to the subject in the form of a new or fresh understanding. Thus, when Christ, world, or man asks for (bids for) something, the respondent has an important choice to make in deciding whether or not to give of himself, to give what has been asked, and so prompt the exchange to go on.

The word "bid" itself recurs often in the poetry, not only in its sense of commanding or asking but in its more worldly meaning, its monetary use, the offering of a price at an auction or sale:

> Buy then! bid then!—What?—Prayer, patience, alms, vows.
>
> ("The Starlight Night")

Here Hopkins takes otherworldly relationships out of their shadowy realm of unknowability and sees them in the familiar marketplace. The aspiring youth has counters of value—"Prayer, patience, alms, vows"—with which to pay for what he is experiencing and with which to deal for more.

In fact, the metaphor of the marketplace, of trade, appears often within the context of the give-and-take relationship. In an early poem, complaining of unrequited love, the speaker says, "My bankrupt heart has no more tears to spend" ("The Beginning of the End"). Later, the metaphor is translated into another context and becomes far more subtle. Finding God, the getting of grace, earning one's way to heaven: They are all serious business, the important transactions, with characteristic trade-offs and risks, gains and losses. In the mature poetry the metaphor is usually subordinated to another and never obtrusive:

> Generations have trod, have trod, have trod;
>   And all is seared with trade; bleared, smeared with toil;
>   And wears man's smudge and shares man's smell: the soil
> Is bare now, nor can foot feel, being shod.

> And for all this, nature is never spent;
>
> ("God's Grandeur")

When Hopkins writes "And for all this, nature is never spent," he is using "spent" in an implied sexual sense (nature as generative), saying that nature is never completely exhausted or used up; at the same time, "spent" retains its monetary meaning because "all this"—the forces seeking to destroy nature's creativity and grandeur—includes the fact that man has burnt or seared the world "with trade."

The metaphors of creativity and business are similarly mixed in "Thou art indeed just, Lord." The speaker complains that his returns have not justified his outlay, that his business has not prospered (line three) as sinners' ways do. The metaphor continues:

> Oh, the sots and thralls of lust
> Do in spare hours more thrive than I that spend,

> Sir, life upon thy cause.

Immediately after this, "thrive" returns to its more natural setting as the speaker looks at the flowering of nature about him and then asks for the life-giving rain of grace. As he makes the turn to the natural imagery of the world, "banks" may be transitional, glancing back for a bare instant at the monetary imagery even as it pulls us forward firmly into the natural world:

> Oh, the sots and thralls of lust
> Do in spare hours more thrive than I that spend,
>
> Sir, life upon thy cause. See, banks and brakes
> Now, leavèd how thick! lacèd they are again
> With fretty chervil, look, and fresh wind shakes
>
> Them;

In both "God's Grandeur" and "Thou art indeed just, Lord," the negative vocabulary of business slips away, displaced by the generative nature to which it leads.

Hopkins' use of the marketplace turns on its association with the getting of value and valuables; trade in the marketplace closes in on the traditional words of love. The association is clearest in "The Handsome Heart," a poem which contrasts the two purchases (of 'goods' and of 'the good'). The child's goodness buys him heaven when he forgoes the choice of a worldly present:

> 'But tell me, child, your choice; what shall I buy
> You?'—'Father, what you buy me I like best.'
> With the sweetest air that said, still plied and pressed,
> He swung to his first poised purport of reply.

Later in the poem, the speaker's response to the child's words makes the metaphoric connection clear:

> Of heaven what boon to buy you, boy, or gain
> Not granted?—Only . . . O on that path you pace
> Run all your race, O brace sterner that strain!

The monetary imagery is perhaps more traditional in "The Lantern out of Doors," a poem in which men go by, "till death or distance buys them quite." The speaker, trapped in mortal time, is doomed to forget their light, but they are not forgotten:

> Christ minds: Christ's interest, what to avow or amend
>   There, éyes them, heart wánts, care haúnts, foot
>   fóllows kínd,
> Their ránsom, théir rescue, ánd first, fást, last friénd.

That is, Christ ransoms man, or repays man with his interest (in both senses), when man is bought by death or distance—a most literal redemption. 'Redemption' is a word Hopkins generally avoids,[18] but its derivative, "ransom," which may more readily suggest actual payment, figures again in "Felix Randal," where the ransom offered is the communion wafer—a rare coin indeed:

> a heavenlier heart began some
> Months earlier, since I had our sweet reprieve and ransom
> Tendered to him.

"Tendered" is wonderful here, suggesting at once the payment or legal tender, the offering of it, as well as the tenderness of the ransom itself, of the priest who offers it, and of the sick patient who elicits it all.

'Dear,' a word Hopkins used very frequently in the poems,[19] sometimes suggests price as well as affection, although the emphasis seems always on the fondness between speaker and subject. "Felix Randal" continues:

> This seeing the sick endears them to us, us too it endears.

Because the line follows the more explicit, earlier financial imagery, it suggests the very high value or worth of each man to the other: "Endears" comes to mean 'makes more precious' in a literal sense. It is significant that in the line's second half—"us too it endears"— Hopkins leaves the verb without a named indirect object. The line so suggests that we endear ourselves not only to the sick ("them") but to Christ also; as we come to see the weak as endearing, we ourselves become endearing to Christ.

Elsewhere, too, the cost of a spiritual life is dear; the word, while it speaks first to a loving and tender relationship, by means of its context glances at the 'expense' with which such a relationship is bought:

> But he scores it in scarlet himself on his own bespoken,
> Before-time-taken, dearest prizèd and pricèd—
>
> *(Deutschland, 22)*

And what is Earth's eye, tongue, or heart else, where
Else, but in dear and dogged man?—Ah, the heir
                                    ("Ribblesdale")

    'Duly, dear Lord, my prize is won.
    I did repent; I am forgiven.
    Give him the gift.'
                        ("A Voice from the World")

As the last excerpt suggests, there is always that within man's relationship to God which escapes the metaphor of exchange, for man is trying to 'buy' far more than he can 'pay' for. So, after his enthusiastic description of the night, the speaker of "The Starlight Night" concludes that "it is all a purchase, all is a prize." The prize goes beyond what has been given in exchange, perhaps suggesting too the element of chance involved in the enterprise. Prizing things figures into "The Golden Echo" too: "Where whatever's prizèd and passes of us, everything that's fresh and fast flying of us, seems to us sweet of us and swiftly away with, done away with, undone." In this poem, too, the young have "winning ways," just as in "Spring" the innocent boy and girl are "worthy the winning." (In context, this last phrase is especially deft in its suggestion of "winnowing," the method of Christ's winning.) The Eurydice's human cargo is its true "lade and treasure"; "Penmaen Pool" invites the reader to "spend" there his "measure of time and treasure."

The language of prizes and treasure, rather conventional in religious poetry, strays only a little from the more striking and literal metaphor of trade. The marketplace is factual and direct, empirically familiar to all in everyday dealing. With it, the poet speaks to the reality and accessibility of God in the world. The metaphor, like the imperative, must have come easily to Hopkins, Victorian son of a shipping insurance man. But it goes further and is especially apt because, rather than suggesting the mystical nature of man's relation to God, trade posits an exchange, a trans-*action*. Finally, that the trade metaphor recurs may lend clarity and reality to the much more traditional imagery of treasure and treasuring, of wealth and riches, of precious metals and jewels.[20]

Hopkins' use of the trade metaphor is part of his continued attempt to realize God in the world. His use of the imperative, in its sharp, clear definition of what man's response to God should be, also strives hard to make God close, knowable, and real. The verbs that bid and the metaphor of bidding increase our sense of the poetry's activity, its struggle to be part of the world. From one point of view, the poetry of Hopkins is a record of interaction undergone; from another, however, it is bidding that similar interaction recur, the imperative assuming its worldly place as an impetus to that action, and the metaphor of trade insisting that we are all familiar with the way to proceed: "Buy then! bid then!"

The exclamation is another readily identifiable characteristic of Hopkins' syntax: "Thou mastering me / God!" The opening of *The Wreck of the Deutschland* is not a prayer that something happen but something happening now and with force. The violence is not a desired possibility but an established—and experienced—fact. That is, the startling opening of the poem that begins Hopkins' mature work has us listening to a speaker plunged into the middle of an experience. The line subordinates and engulfs the speaker in the naming of the God who is the subject and the verb, and the beginning and the end, of the exclamation. It does this even as it asserts a very personal relationship between the speaker and his God: The "me" that is so subordinated, caught between its namings of God, remains the direct object of God's action in the here and now.

The active violence of Hopkins' imagery has often reminded readers of John Donne's poetry,[21] but again the differences of tone, and of the self seen in relation to God's violence, are as striking as the similarities. Donne does invoke the God of the *Deutschland* when he asks for violence and tension as a means of reaching heaven:

Batter my heart, three person'd God; for, you
As yet but knocke, breathe, shine, and seeke to mend;

That I may rise, and stand, o'erthrow mee, 'and bend
Your force, to breake, blowe, burn and make me new.

For all the force of his lists of verbs, Donne's imperative remains a prayer, a plea. Moreover, unlike Hopkins' first person, the "I" of the Donne poem is a universal "I," unparticularized and stretching out to become all 'I's.' In fact, Donne's "I" turns into a communal structure in the elaborate metaphor of the "usurpt towne" that follows. Hopkins, in voicing a very similar relationship, leaves not nearly so much space for the reader to identify with the speaker: "Thou mastering me / God!" So Hopkins' speaker makes us know his own uniqueness even as he begins. Although mastered, although caught as the direct object of God's attention, that speaker is not passive: His exclamatory words voice his intense excitement and activity in response.

The exclamation recurs frequently in Hopkins, probably more frequently than in any other major English poet. At its best, the mark seems inevitable, the expected end emerging from an excited or impassioned voice already heard within the language. At other times, the mark seems no more than Hopkins' way of emphasizing or underlining the verse—another attempt, like the externally imposed stress marks of sprung rhythm, to point out the words to be stressed, the rhythms and tempos that the poet is hearing. Even so, like Emily Dickinson's dashes, Hopkins' exclamations much affect our hearing of the poem and its tone. The exclamations always heighten the pitch of the speaker's voice. They may increase the tempo and act as rhythmical guides, demanding a marked, if short, pause. They may even affect our hearing of the voice's volume. First and last, since they signal excitement, they suggest spontaneity of language on the speaker's part. As such, they temper the dense patterns of sound, the conscious and forethought language. That is, what seems to be unpremeditated tempers what seems to be artful and consciously crafted, and the poem transmits energy in the subtle activity of play between the two distinctions of voice.

The exclamations in "The Starlight Night" follow so closely on one another that they seem self-engendering:

Look at the stars! look, look up at the skies!
    O look at all the fire-folk sitting in the air!
    The bright boroughs, the circle-citadels there!
Down in dim woods the diamond delves! the elves'-eyes!
The grey lawns cold where gold, where quickgold lies!
    Wind-beat whitebeam! airy abeles set on a flare!
    Flake-doves sent floating forth at a farmyard scare!—
Ah well! it is all a purchase, all is a prize.

    Buy then! bid then!—What?—Prayer, patience, alms, vows.
    Look, look: a May-mess, like on orchard boughs!
        Look! March-bloom, like on mealed-with-yellow sallows!
    These are indeed the barn; withindoors house
    The shocks. This piece-bright paling shuts the spouse
        Christ home, Christ and his mother and all his hallows.

Although the length of the phrases in the octave varies considerably, the effect of the exclamation marks is difficult to sustain, and the tone seems somewhat strained after the first quatrain. At the same time, the alternatives—semicolons or dashes—would have made the poem far less electric and far less urgent both here and in the later force of the sestet. The octave's effect is iconographic with the exclamations marking sight as an activity while the words catalogue the things that are sighted. The "Ah well!" at the end of the octave marks a turning, a motion of resignation that turns away from the world and moves back into the mind. It prepares us for the thought that holds the octave's pictures together: "Ah well! it is all a purchase, all is a prize."

The voice of the sestet masters both rhythm and mood, the colloquial variation of syntax carrying the reader easily. "Buy then! bid then!" is the imperative response to the seen world just before that world grasps the speaker's attention again, pulling him back sharply to the dynamic world: "Look, look: a May-mess, like on orchard boughs! / Look! March-bloom, like on mealed-with-yellow sallows!" Still it is the last tercet, the close of the poem, that quiets all uneasiness and brings the tone to rest. The delicate flashings of nature are seen to "withindoors house" Christ and family, and this final revelation unfolds without the surface excitement of exclamation marks:

> These are indeed the barn; withindoors house
> The shocks. This piece-bright paling shuts the spouse
> Christ home, Christ and his mother and all his hallows.

In these lines, the speaker discovers the meaning and pierces the surface excitement of the world as the language moves beyond physical description to meditation, the meaning read. The ending deepens the poem as it penetrates further into both mind and world. We are moved from the dynamic sharpness of the world to its calm and indwelling wonder. The poem makes much of its statement through the use of exclamations and then makes its more profound statement through the conscious lack of them. The final excitement passes beyond excitement and into still wonder. And Hopkins presents that final explanation—that Christ, Mary, and saints are the indwelling principle of the world's beauty—as fact, as simple, syntactically clear statement.

This pattern is repeated in other poems. Hopkins often saves the most telling thought, the deepest insight, for last, and the poems rarely end in exclamation. When it follows anything more substantial than an interjected word of amazement ("Oh!" or "Ah!"), the exclamation mark often stresses the surface excitement of natural beauty, the world's loveliness. But at the poem's end, the understanding reached signifies a deeper penetration, and the final understanding is the firmer because of the preceding exclamations. Thus, the sighting of the immortal diamond is not an exclamation but a sustained and controlled assertion:

>   Enough! the Resurrection,
> A heart's-clarion! Away grief's gasping, ׀ joyless days, dejection.
>   Across my foundering deck shone
> A beacon, an eternal beam. ׀ Flesh fade, and mortal trash
> Fall to the residuary worm; ׀ world's wildfire, leave but ash:
>   In a flash, at a trumpet crash,

I am all at once what Christ is, ⹀ since he was what I am, and
This Jack, joke, poor potsherd, ⹀ patch, matchwood, immortal
    diamond,
                  Is immortal diamond.
            ("That Nature is a Heraclitean Fire")

Like the imperative verbs, the exclamations in Hopkins signal the
speaker's activity, his immediacy in the poem. Often, they seem to
mark his impatience with traditional syntax and with the conven-
tional lengthy phrases used to define relationships. Instead, as in
"The Starlight Night," we read lists of exclaimed nouns—things
out there in the world, things so striking and compelling that they
consume attention and momentarily displace conventional modes
of written language. In the exclamation, Hopkins again found a
structure that he could use to imply the forcefulness and physicality
of God's presence in the world as well as the spontaneity and
excitement of the speaker who reacts to that presence. From the
reader, the exclamation asks a forceful reaction, demands a con-
centration of self and energy rising in response to the represented
world.

If the reader can presumably follow the speaker into exclamation
on the world's wonder, it is harder to re-enact the exclamation
with which Hopkins marks the single instant of breathlessness—
the interjection.[22] For the speaker, the interjection signals an emo-
tional intervention—the emotion responding to and at the under-
standing of the design that has not yet found the language to say
itself—and allows for the gathering of the mind's conscious powers
before the resumption of meaningful word order:

          Ah! there was a heart right!
                   (*Deutschland, 29*)

Let him oh! with his air of angels then lift me, lay me!
                            ("Henry Purcell")

Áh! ás the heart grows older
It will come to such sights colder
("Spring and Fall")

The 'ahs' and 'ohs' stand apart from their argumentative, narrative, or descriptive contexts. Although the reader is surely meant to penetrate their surface, to feel the emotion of the speaker, and the fact that what is about to emerge has great importance, the exclamations themselves are without denotative referential meaning. Yet it is precisely in these dislocating motions of language that the distinctive drama of the poems is enacted, making acutely present the hidden activity of the speaker's inner experience. The drama is complex, for the speaker is now simultaneously responding to both inner and outer worlds, concurrently finding language that will convey the mind's activity in its grasping for appropriate language, but also finding language that will allow the resumption of traditional modes of discourse.

Since they have no referential meaning and so interrupt the flow of intelligible argument, exclaimed interjections are especially striking when the poetry's language is crammed, dense with meaning, word, and interwoven sound:

Because the Holy Ghost over the bent
World broods with warm breast and with ah! bright wings.
("God's Grandeur")

The clause is lengthy and without a marked stop (other than the exclamation) at which the voice can rest. The texture of sound, with its recurring and transferring '*b*'s,' '*w*'s,' and '*r*'s,' is as complex and intertwined as is imaginable. Within this complexity of sound and language, the lyrical "ah!" seems to release everything—to be a foreshadowing in the speaker's language of the still potential flight of "bright wings." The "ah!" exclaims at and in the vision—the visionary understanding—that has come: A pause precedes it, and then the open vowel sound slowly dies, readying the reader for the lightness, the transcendence, of the rising end of the poem, the dawn.

The speaker's "ah" is then far different from the reader's, for the reader is only being readied, has not yet seen or even begun to see what is gathering before the speaker. The reader can only intuit the wonder of what is to come; for him, the interjection is a sign of emotion and anticipation, another of Hopkins' directional signals but as yet without intelligible reference. The speaker is before the vision in space, searching out the language perhaps to say the sudden shining clarity; but the reader is before it in time, knowing only that what is to come has been strong enough to dissipate wholly the dense and rapid tide of lyrical language preceding it. In the exclaimed interjection, then, Hopkins again dramatically alters the tempo of language and again separates speaker from reader, insisting on differentiating the reader's response even as he bids the reader more fully into the experience of the poem.

Hopkins is so direct, so active in his responses and so eager to see God in the world, that it comes as some surprise to see how often the question mark occurs in his poetry. The questions in Hopkins may not stand out in the reader's mind in the way that the exclamations or interjections do probably because the questions rarely remain real questions—they rarely hang unanswered. Again, although his subject is by definition unknowable, Hopkins manages to suggest that, for all practical purposes, the earnest questioner can find the right answers without difficulty. Whether his speaker poses his questions to man, God, or self, the answer is soon forthcoming:

> What is all this juice and all this joy?
>   A strain of the earth's sweet being in the beginning
> In Eden garden.
>
> ("Spring")

> Buy then! bid then!—What?—Prayer, patience, alms, vows.
> ("The Starlight Night")

> Why, tears! is it? tears; such a melting, a madrigal start!
> (*Deutschland, 18*)

> Question: What is Spring?—
> Growth in everything—
>
> ("The May Magnificat")

> —Where kept? do but tell us where kept, where.—
> Yonder.—What high as that! We follow, now we follow.—
> Yonder, yes yonder, yonder,
> Yonder.
>
> ("The Golden Echo")

> 'But tell me, child, your choice; what shall I buy
> You?'—'Father what you buy me I like best.'
> With the sweetest air that said, still plied and pressed,
> He swung to his first poised purport of reply.
>
> ("The Handsome Heart")

The speaker's prompt responses to the questions he himself has just asked are definite and emphasized. Indeed, the question's nearness to the exclamation comes clear in the excerpts quoted from "The Golden Echo" and the *Deutschland*, in which the exclamation marks could have easily been question marks. And even when the question entails real conflict for Hopkins, it does not often betray conflict on the page.

Hopkins fully recognized the conflict inherent in his love for beauty and his love for God. Speaking of human beauty, he wrote to Bridges, "I think . . . no one can admire beauty of the body more than I do. . . . But this kind of beauty is dangerous."[23] In "To what serves Mortal Beauty?" Hopkins' speaker goes so far as to confront that problem and 'solve' it. The poem begins with question and answer:

> To what serves mortal beauty | —dangerous; does set danc-
> ing blood—the O-seal-that-so | feature, flung prouder form
> Than Purcell tune lets tread to? | See: it does this: keeps warm
> Men's wits to the things that are; | what good means—where
>   a glance
> Master more may than gaze, | gaze out of countenance.

Later, in the sestet, the answers come even more decisively:

> Our law says: Love what are ⏐ love's worthiest, were
>   all known;
> World's loveliest—men's selves. Self ⏐ flashes off frame and
>   face.
> What do then? how meet beauty? ⏐ Merely meet it; own,
> Home at heart, heaven's sweet gift; ⏐ then leave, let that alone.
> Yea, wish that though, wish all, ⏐ God's better beauty, grace.

The answer is both simple and neat. One must "meet" beauty, "own" (in both senses) it as a gift from God, and "then leave, let that alone."²⁴ The conflict is solved, and the question answered, by the speaker's simple imperative demand for abstinence from that which he has been at such pains to justify as potentially good. One may enjoy beauty, he says, but only for a certain time and to a certain degree, by glance and not by gaze. "Then leave, let that alone": Is it because of the abruptness of this phrase that the poem's last line then doubles back to qualify or soften the order to put mortal beauty aside? Perhaps, yet the line itself—"Yea, wish that though, wish all, ⏐ God's better beauty, grace"—recognizes no uncertainty. Indeed, the rhythms of the last tercet are varied and graceful. The answer emerges in the sureness of a string of imperatives, and the lines are far clearer in syntax, diction, and sound than any others in the poem:

> What do then? how meet beauty? ⏐ Merely meet it; own,
> Home at heart, heaven's sweet gift; ⏐ then leave, let that alone.
> Yea, wish that though, wish all, ⏐ God's better beauty, grace.

In other words, in spite of whatever hesitation is betrayed by the speaker's motion of mind or by the adequacy of the answer he proposes, that answer emerges as commandingly, and as didactically, as all the other answers in Hopkins.

Even more sure of itself than the question with an immediate answer is the rhetorical question, the question answered by the very fact of its having been asked:

Márgarét, áre you gríeving
Over Goldengrove unleaving?

("Spring and Fall")

What would the world be, once bereft
Of wet and of wildness?

("Inversnaid")

What hinders? Are you beam-blind, yet to a fault
In a neighbour deft-handed? Are you that liar
And, cast by conscience out, spendsavour salt?

("The Candle Indoors")

There was single eye!
Read the unshapeable shock night
And knew the who and the why;
Wording it how but by him that present and past,
Heaven and earth are word of, worded by?—

(Deutschland, 29)

has wilder, wilful-wavier
Meal-drift moulded ever and melted across skies?

("Hurrahing in Harvest")

In these examples, the rhetorical question performs much the same
function as the exclamation does: A tonal device, it defines more
sharply the speaker's voice for the reader. The rhetorical question
makes us know the speaker's amazement, his wonder, his near-
disbelief in confronting the certainty he has come upon.

The pattern of question and answer is a recurring turn of mind
in the poems. So sure does the reader become in reading Hopkins'
questions that they rarely render mystery, uncertainty, or even
great pause. With a few significant exceptions, the questions in
the finished poems are never really directed at the self or at the
reader the way the imperatives are. Ironically, the question most
often indicates the settled mind of the speaker rather than his
perplexity or irresolution. They are, finally, the questions of a
catechism with ready, immediately declared answers. Like the boy

in "The Handsome Heart," Hopkins' speaker seems to swing easily to his "first poised purport of reply."

But whatever the poetry may here sacrifice in depth, it gains in the assurance of its reader. We come to read in confident expectation that the speaker's answer will be explicit. The questions then become another and more subtle form of the bidding to right action, direction, or thought. Finally, the recurring pattern of question and answer forms yet another structure that signals the speaker's exactitude, his sureness, and most of all, his belief in a continuously responsive universe.

In "The Leaden Echo and the Golden Echo," paired question-and-answer poems, the speaker does find—at first—the wrong answer. (The poems were intended as a chorus in a drama, and the speaker is not Hopkins' usual speaker.) The poems, exploring human mutability, ask if there is a way to hold on to beauty. The answer of no, in the first poem, yields to the golden echo of "spare" within the earlier "despair": Beauty can be saved—and man with it. Beauty given back to God is kept by God "yonder." The answers are both offered didactically. The difference between them comes from hearing the word's echo. Together, the poems are a kind of dialogue of body and soul, a dialogue which makes its point by the contrasting moods the two answers provoke. The poems form a dialogue but not a dialectic, and this not merely because of the one-sided point of view in each: The flatness, repetition, and godlessness of "The Leaden Echo" make the further answer of "The Golden Echo" inevitable in Hopkins.

With extreme self-confidence and self-assurance, Hopkins' speaker continues to ask and be answered throughout the poems. In one poem, "The Soldier," he affirms that he has found the right answer before he reveals the question:

> Yes. Whý do we áll, seeing of a soldier, bless him? bless
> Our redcoats, our tars? Both these being, the greater part,
> But frail clay, nay but foul clay. Here it is: the heart,
> Since, proud, it calls the calling manly, gives a guess
> That, hopes that, makesbelieve, the men must be no less;

The opening "Yes" declares the surety of the answer before the question and answer are framed. "Here it is:" the speaker proclaims, offering the answer, enclosing the question in his own certainty of what must follow. The answer itself snaps to a conclusion in its multiple rhyming of "less" with "guess" and "bless,"— and both words (and answer) are the firmer for their rhyming with the original "Yes." What the speaker gives as reason for man's admiration of the soldier, he later further affirms by showing us Christ bending down in response to that soldier—which is to say *acting* out, as well as saying, the same admiration:

> For love he leans forth, needs his neck must fall on, kiss,
> And cry 'O Christ-done deed! So God-made-flesh does too:
> Were I come o'er again' cries Christ 'it should be this'.

That question and answer are self-conscious repetitions of what is already known is suggested by all their uses but is made most manifest in "The Soldier." Hopkins' answers are a priori, preexistent, and ordained in the world; they need only be 'read' right. His belief in a responsive universe shapes a structural pattern of syntax that responds to question with certain answer. "A Catholic by mystery," Hopkins explains to Bridges, "means an incomprehensible certainty: without certainty, without formulation there is no interest."[25] In the poems, the formulation of answer is so certain and so certainly to come that the reader learns to pause hardly at all between question and answer. The syntactical pattern varies the rhythm, speed, and tone of the poem, again marking dynamic changes, but the mystery that a question mark might suggest is always subordinate to the certainty of the answer.

As the question bids the reader strongly onward, it again separates him from the speaker, leaving him waiting for the answer the speaker already knows—the answer that he knows the speaker already knows. Yet if the question-as-question is not strongly directed at the reader, the answer is; the answer is more pointedly set out for our consideration. "Here it is": The speaker offers his prepared response as if on a platter, inviting the reader's admiration, bidding him to realize his own selfhood anew through the further response of differentiated assent.

The imperative verb, the exclamation, the interjection, and the question and answer are all forceful patterns of syntax, breaking out from the declarative sentence so strongly and so frequently that they constitute much of what we know as the singular, bidding voice of Hopkins. But the patterns are not unrelieved. Like the motions of self outward and upward in assent and the directed patterns of lyricism and design, Hopkins' patterns of syntax show extreme variation, variation that turns customary practice upside down or flees into another country entirely. Again we know the depth of the speaker's dark emotion at least in part by realizing how far he has traveled from the syntactical habits of language so firmly established.

Nowhere is the distance more evident than in Hopkins' use of the question. Only in deep disconsolation, in the sonnets of desolation for example, and in a telling fragment of a play—a soliloquy spoken by a murderer—do the speaker's questions suggest the impossibility of answer; only in desolation do the questions come forth into an uncertain and unresponsive world. Hopkins wrote about a few of these poems:

> These came like inspirations unbidden and against my will. And in the life I lead now, which is one of continually jaded and harassed mind, if in any leisure I try to do anything I make no way—nor with my work, alas! but so it must be.[26]

The sonnets of desolation enact this feeling of harassment, so their questions are of a whole other order. Here, the questions are not only unanswered but seemingly wholly unanswerable:

> No worst, there is none. Pitched past pitch of grief,
> More pangs will, schooled at forepangs, wilder wring.
> Comforter, where, where is your comforting?
> Mary, mother of us, where is your relief?
>
> ("No worst, there is none")

The certainty we have come to know and trust in other poems magnifies the sense of loss endured; "beginning to despair," the speaker now reveals no hint of any golden echo to come. The traditional imperatives of litany become a helpless questioning, a litany of anguish. The voice seems to reach, as if out of habit, for an answer, as if to find what has always been the joy of response; but finding no response it falls back into a density, both linguistic and imagistic, which can only describe the questioning itself:

> My cries heave, herds-long; huddle in a main, a chief-
> woe, world-sorrow; on an age-old anvil wince and sing—

A willful intervention is needed to break out of the solipsistic force of these heavy, compounded redundancies; implicitly, the relief sought is from the interminable, tormenting questioning which finds no response:

> Then lull, then leave off. Fury had shrieked 'No ling-
> ering! Let me be fell: force I must be brief'.

Unlike the questions with their a priori answers in other parts of the Hopkins canon, the questioning in the sonnets of desolation is a sign of the interior drama of the speaker, of the mind's activity and dark energies. In fact, the questioning that finds no release in a confirming response not only creates a tension in the poem, but, because it is so much in conflict with the formulated patterns of questioning in the other poems, creates a kind of subsidiary drama within the canon. Possibly implied in the questioning in these sonnets is the idea that the process itself may be ameliorative; that, as in Tennyson, "a use in measured language lies." But in fact the language and the depth of despair it seeks to measure and portray remain unmeasurable:

> O the mind, mind has mountains; cliffs of fall
> Frightful, sheer, no-man-fathomed. Hold them cheap
> May who ne'er hung there. Nor does long our small
> Durance deal with that steep or deep.

The original question 'where?' is lost, repressed when the process of questioning itself threatens to overcome the questioner. But although displaced, a kind of response re-emerges in the conclusion. The conclusion, forged out of the poem's own processes of repressed questioning, fails to find the answer it sought; that is, it fails to 'read' a pre-existent and definitive response emerging from the world:

> Here! creep,
> Wretch, under a comfort serves in a whirlwind: all
> Life death does end and each day dies with sleep.

Because the impulse to find an answer has failed, the speaker contemptuously orders himself into whatever unconsciousness he can find. Implicitly, the answer to 'where?' is no where, no place— but the very thought of ultimate conclusion becomes a kind of temporary dwelling, reminiscent of Lear on the heath, an idea at least of ending the process of tormented questioning, but in an unknowable and unlocatable place. No less than in any other poem, there is a presumption that there are answers, but like God's grace they are now unlocatable and unforthcoming.

The question of existent answer is contained, too, in the imagery's repeated allusions to biblical passages.[27] The allusions suggest that the poem's speaker is not unique in his experience of anguish and that salvation is yet possible. At the same time, the allusions are but whispers in the poem and go all unacknowledged, seemingly unread, by the speaker. In more than one way, his agony emerges from a deep sense that the answers, once ready, have been lost. For the speaker of "No worst, there is none," the sense of a sympathetic universe responsive to God has been lost. There is no reciprocity to be had, and the speaker's self-contempt for his failure to find an answer continues in the irresolution of an ending that has not even begun to satisfy the questions asked. For Hopkins, there is a very real sense in which God is not the mystery; the lack of him is.

In a long fragment of the poetic drama "St. Winefred's Well," Hopkins explores the thought processes of Caradoc, murderer of Winefred, just after his crime. Caradoc's soliloquy, seventy lines long, is closely related to the sonnets of desolation in its time of composition, in its language, and in its tone.[28] The soliloquy begins with a series of questions revealing Caradoc's wonderment, a disbelief born of horror at what he has done:

> My héart, where have we been? | What have we séen, my
> mind?
> What stroke has Carádoc's right arm dealt? | what done?
> Head of a rebel
> Struck óff it has; written | upon lovely limbs,
> In bloody letters, lessons | of earnest, of revenge;

The answer to his questions, as fearful and as unimaginable as it seems to him, is already fact and "written" in blood. In his distraction, Caradoc strives to deny the undeniable, and his next set of questions, in refusing to believe the deed he knows he has done, ironically inverts Hopkins' more usual rhetorical questions:

> What work? what harm's done? There is | no harm done,
> none yet;
> Perhaps we struck no blow, | Gwenvrewi lives perhaps;

But his action is pre-existent and irrevocable, and Caradoc is drawn back into the whirlpool of memory, envisioning again her dissevered head.

Since his attempt to deny his action fails, Caradoc must either admit guilt or affirm his deed. Trapped, he is drawn further into sin, defiantly declaring himself his own god:

> What is virtue? Valour; | only the heart valiant.
> And right? Only resolution; | will, his will unwavering

The process of mind here is a perversion of the process of questioning in the earlier poems. Here the answers arrive just as quickly as they do there; they exist a priori within the speaker, but they are blatantly wrong, proceeding from a heart determined to cut itself off from God, humanity, and world. Even Caradoc knows that his answers are too opposed to human nature to work, that his body lives in the self-same mutable world he would deny. The terrifying questions that undercut his resolve arise unbidden, and for a moment, Caradoc becomes human as he reveals his own sense of helplessness:

> But wíll flesh, O can flésh
> Second this fiery strain? | Not always; O no no!
> We cannot live this life out; | sometimes we must weary
> And in this darksome world | what comfort can I find?
> Down this darksome world | cómfort whére can I find
> When 'ts light I quenched;

Almost immediately, language takes over, swelling the first question into the more desperate revisionary question: "But wíll flesh, O can flésh / Second this fiery strain?" His answer, implicit in the repetition of "flesh," moves from a tentative no to an absolute one.

When the speaker of "No worst, there is none" cries "Comforter, where, where is your comforting?" he is in torment, but there is yet hope of finding relief. Even in the bleak desolation of "I wake and feel," the speaker concludes, "The lost are like this . . . but worse." In Caradoc, Hopkins goes a further step, trying on the voice of a persona who allows himself to admit that he *is* lost, a persona who insists on being damned and so cuts off even the faintest hope of being saved. It is Hopkins' vision of hell on earth, a didacticism of evil. Caradoc casts his questions out vainly, damning himself with his pride as surely as he did with his murder of Gwenvrewi. Although his words echo those of "No worst, there is none," his question is significantly different: "*what* comfort can I find? / *Down* this darksome *world* | cómfort whére can I find / When 'ts light I quenched" (italics added). The question *is* a question, and it does reveal the human vulnerability that his proud bravado had sought to conceal, but the opening or possibility for change is at last clamped shut, for Caradoc's eye is trained in the wrong direction.

Predictably, the loss of Gwenvrewi felt again does not change Caradoc. It does, however, somewhat temper his spirited self-assurance, and at the end his pride is still defiant but now resign-

edly so. The opening in the question, which for a moment might
have led to a real turning, is not allowed to do so; his future is
terrible, no future at all. His soul, he sees, "Must all day long
taste murder." His final questions are dismissed out of hand—
questioning itself is dismissed:

> What do nów then? Do? Nay,
> Déed-bound I am; óne deed tréads all dówn here ᴵ

He is, he says, not allowed even to think of alternatives, for no
change is possible. Hopkins' understanding of the psychological ef-
fects of sin is acute. Concluding himself trapped, Caradoc despairs:

> Déed-bound I am; óne deed tréads all dówn here ᴵ cramps
>   all doing. What do? Not yield,
> Not hope, not pray; despair; ᴵ ay, that: brazen despair out,
> Brave all, and take what comes—

The repetition of "What do?" is mocking repetition, and his an-
swer, foreordained by sin, is clogged with negatives; only the sin
of despair emerges in positive form.

The end of the soliloquy foretells the physical death consequent
upon the spiritual death we have witnessed:

> Brave all, and take what comes— ᴵ as here this rabble is come,
> Whose bloods I reck no more of, ᴵ no more rank with hers
> Than sewers with sacred oils. ᴵ Mankind, that mob, comes.
>   Come!

That final, flung imperative "Come!" constitutes an ironic inver-
sion of the nun's triumphant cry at death, " 'O Christ, Christ,
come quickly' " (*Deutschland*, 24). Caradoc's cry willfully wel-
comes human violence, death, and damnation. Only for a moment
was there the slightest hint that salvation and change might yet
be possible. The question at the center—"And in this darksome
world ᴵ what comfort can I find?"—is that hint, quickly repudiated
by Caradoc. Caught in the mire he has himself created, Caradoc's
other rhetorical questions are devilish in the answers they take for

granted. At the end he has nothing to care for and nothing to lose; his demise is reck-less of both man and God.

"Carrion Comfort" opens with a quatrain that, although reminiscent of Caradoc's soliloquy in its language, shows the self rising in answer to the dangerous allure of despair. The sonnet's dramatic opening posits a speaker directly responding to the personified Despair:

> Not, I'll not, carrion comfort, Despair, not feast on thee;
> Not untwist—slack they may be—these last strands of man
> In me ór, most weary, cry *I can no more*. I can;
> Can something, hope, wish day come, not choose not to be.

The speaker's last three words echo Hamlet's question in soliloquy, but Hopkins' speaker, even when so dispirited, knows what the answer ought to be. Incapable of enacting the right answer, he asserts that he is yet able to refuse to enact the wrong one. He asserts that he will yet negate the temptation of the negatives, that there is—or must be—some positive left to him. ("I can; / Can something, hope, wish day come, not choose not to be" contrasts sharply with Caradoc's resolution, "What do? Not yield, / Not hope, not pray; despair; ' ay, that.") If the opening of "Carrion Comfort" is some answer, however inadequate, the rest of the poem constitutes a drama of successive questions displacing earlier ones:

> But ah, but O thou terrible, why wouldst thou rude on me
> Thy wring-world right foot rock? lay a lionlimb against me?
>   scan
> With darksome devouring eyes my bruisèd bones? and fan,
> O in turns of tempest, me heaped there; me frantic to avoid
>   thee and flee?

By the end of this second quatrain, the speaker has shifted his focus from present to past, distancing himself and his extremity of pain in time and space through imaginative image ("me heaped there"). The pictures have become more fearsome, and the questions, real questions, more rapid in their succession, yet now, possibly because of the distancing, a turning point has been reached.

When the "Why?" recurs at the start of the sestet, it at last finds an answer, however partial. The speaker pulls forward, still on uncertain ground, revising and qualifying his answer, slowly finding his way toward the larger conclusion he hopes for:

> Why? That my chaff might fly; my grain lie, sheer and clear.
> Nay in all that toil, that coil, since (seems) I kissed the rod,
> Hand rather, my heart lo! lapped strength, stole joy, would
> laugh, chéer.

As the questions begin to find answers, the speaker becomes more and more eager, seemingly trembling on the brink of discovery. The answers seem to be breeding questions as energetically as the questions do answers. In fact, the questions are themselves tentatively hopeful answers, measuring the distance the speaker has traveled since the sonnet's start:

> Cheer whom though? The hero whose heaven-handling flung
> me, fóot tród
> Me? or me that fought him? O which one? is it each one?
> That night, that year
> Of now done darkness I wretch lay wrestling with (my God!)
> my God.

Like the question of 'where?' in "No worst, there is none," the question of "Why?" in "Carrion Comfort" enacts the speaker's interior drama. And as in "No worst, there is none," the conclusion of "Carrion Comfort" emerges from the poem's own processes and not as a sign emerging from the world. But "Carrion Comfort" finds affirmative response. Its questioning becomes questing because its questions are not repressed but eagerly engender other questions. Although its questions appear increasingly retrograde, searching the past, its motion becomes, as the growing urgency and velocity of its questioning suggest, progressive. Meaning, finally, is located in the past:

That night, that year
Of now done darkness I wretch lay wrestling with (my God!)
my God.

It is a recovery of what was lost: in its own way a pre-existent answer, one that could not be 'read' but had to be reached. Beyond this, the loss is made present, "(my God!)" recognized as coming in revelation even before the loss is fully restored—"my God."

"Carrion Comfort" is something of an anomaly for Hopkins, coming to its wonder of revelation through questions born of agony. In others of the sonnets of desolation, the voice begins and ends with itself, for all the wildness of imagery locked in an airless room. The speaker's inability to escape his own despondent self is overpowering. He finds himself bereft of God's imperative, the world's bidding, and all possibility of interaction. "To seem the stranger lies my lot, my life" is so trapped within itself that it uses no less than fifteen first-person pronouns in fourteen lines. The poem thus tells its grief by the heavy burden of selfhood it contains. The speaker uses no questions or imperatives, each of the seven sentences ending with a bleak and unregenerative finality. The syntax betrays an atypical lack of energy.

In "I wake and feel," the exclaimed interjection, which we have seen so often leap up with the speaker's joy, stresses instead his sense of helplessness:

And my lament
Is cries countless, cries like dead letters sent
To dearest him that lives alas! away.

The interjected "alas!" stops us before the line ending, as did the "ah!" before "bright wings" in "God's Grandeur"; but now the line ending, "away," the object of the interjection's emotion, signals a loss, a flight not on the existing edge of sight but out of sight. "Alas!" calls only an awful absence. Hopkins' habit of concreteness is still at work as he turns his communication with God into a literal correspondence, but as in other sonnets of desolation, the answer is unforthcoming. Worse: The responder is absent, and the exchange is rendered impossible.[29]

Even the trade metaphor undergoes an ironic inversion in the sonnets which "came like inspirations unbidden":

> Only what word
>
> Wisest my heart breeds dark heaven's baffling ban
> Bars or hell's spell thwarts. This to hoard unheard,
> Heard unheeded, leaves me a lonely began.
>
> ("To seem the stranger")

The speaker suggests his word, his single coin of exchange, may even be being 'hoarded,' a word that implies selfishness, stagnancy, and a withering (hoary) lack of activity. With its clustered consonants and thudding stress patterns, "dark heaven's baffling ban / Bars or hell's spell thwarts" suggests the absolute density of the obstacles thrust against the speaker's attempt to reach out of himself into the world. In Hopkins' world—a world that wants to say everything "right *to* or *at* the hearer, interesting him, holding him in the attitude of correspondent or addressed or at least concerned"—in Hopkins' world, a word "unheard" or "unheeded" (and here certainly unanswered) is indeed numbing.

Earlier in "To seem the stranger," the speaker countered England's deafness to his cries with a blank assertion: "plead nor do I." The imperative is lost to him, and that too is pain. That there seems no interaction, transaction, or communication possible is the essence of his 'stranger-hood.' The poem's pathos is accentuated because the usual structures of language that the speaker generates are all conspicuously absent: the familiar forms of question and ready answer, of imperative bidding that reaches out to the world, of excited exclamatory interjection. "Heaven's baffling ban" contrasts with the banns of marriage that herald union; this "ban" seems to put him in a prison cell and bar all escape from self. It is indeed "baffling"—perplexing to the point of helplessness and frustrating every attempt to find answer or solution. The poem, circling, finds no way out, no presence to which it can assent. At the end he calls himself "a lonely began," and that past-tense verb used as a static noun is, in its weight and sheer finality, positioned like a stone at the poem's close.

Having forged structures and modes of writing that dramatized man's proper reaction to the sense of God's presence in the world, Hopkins, when that sense was lost to him, shapes a poetry different not only in mood and subject but in mode and structure.[30] In the sonnets of desolation he draws on the very writing he had implicitly sought to repudiate. A dense interiority; a centripetal force pulling the speaker progressively further into himself, reflecting a motion of consciousness and language that he is not able to leap out of or up from; unanswerable questions that give rise to no clarities or, indeed, any response at all; a dependence on a consciousness unwilled and undirected: All these things, far more characteristic of expressionistic or Romantic poetry than of Hopkins, appear in the sonnets of desolation. Inevitably, they suggest to the reader another relation to the poems, in many ways leaving him the space to close in on the speaker and his motion of mind. Hopkins wrote, we remember, that the poems "came like inspirations unbidden and against my will." Set in the context of the rest of the Hopkins canon, the sonnets of desolation are twice-over filled with absences, the structures of bidding and response now turned to wholly other use or simply, tragically lost.

IV

Dramas of Time and Loss

Deeply concerned with human loss, the poems of Hopkins will the redemption of loss, directing human experience toward the saving grace of future time. For as the poet bids man to know direction within the world's space, he bids him too to know direction in time. Hopkins' Christian sense of time is always in evidence, reminding us that however unique a given phenomenon may appear, it yet proceeds from time past and foreshadows time future. The design through time gathers the seemingly unique event into enduring principle; the discrete occurrence is reseen in its truer form as a manifestation of recurrence in a Christ-informed world.

That is the represented time of the poem, what the poem says of time. But any poem exists in many times—in the time of its author's making of it and in the time of its reader's reading of it, and both those times in experiential, representational, and historical dimensions. In Hopkins, not the least of these is the experiential time of the speaker and reader. Hopkins enacts his sense of Christ-informed time by using recurrence as a poetic means as well as a thematic element in the poem: For the reader, Hopkins' bold recurrence of sound and rhythm creates known patterns, recognizable design in the temporal experience of the saying. But just as interesting is the speaker's own experiential or enacted time, which sometimes rises up to tense against the recurrence of represented time, creating complex drama indeed.

Hopkins fosters our awareness of experiential time in his determination to be heard and not merely read. "To do the Eurydice any kind of justice," he instructs Bridges, "you must not slovenly read it with the eyes but with your ears, as if the paper were declaiming it at you. . . . Stress is the life of it." Elsewhere, he repeats the exhortation: "but take breath and read it with the ears, as I always wish to be read, and my verse becomes all right."[1] Such comments make explicit a demand inherent in the poetry itself. Filled with recurrent sound, filled with explosive and stressed sound, Hopkins' verses nearly leap off the page in their eagerness to be heard aloud. Indeed, the poetry's adamant and individual sound patterns compose no small part of its power to bid us. The poem is to be read "as if the paper were declaiming it *at*" us. We are forcefully confronted by sound, the poetry's orality signaling its 'reality' and spontaneity.

Any poem read aloud, heard rather than seen, engenders a distinct experience for the reader. Sound makes us aware of time because sound happens only in movement through time; in Walter J. Ong's phrase, sound tells us that something is "going on."[2] Spoken aloud, the poem comes off the page and ceases to be the still icon of a timeless urn; spoken aloud, the poem is a durational happening with beginning and end.

Because it has a defined beginning and end in time, lyric poetry speaks to the sustaining of meaning: What is said resurrects for a moment what has been and what has been said. For a while, too, it further succeeds in delaying the end, in foreclosing on silence. But by its very nature, the poem said aloud also reminds us of loss: What is said is lost in the time of its saying, the beginning implying the end, the moment of silence or non-saying which succeeds all sound. When the poem is sounded aloud, the tension between lastingness and passing, between the continuity of experience and its loss, becomes explicit. In this sense, it may be that the printed page or space of the poem preserves only the possibility of recreation and loss, preserves only the time we must relive and lose. And Hopkins insists that his poems be lifted off the page to become that temporal experience: "My verse is less to be read than heard, as I have told you before."[3]

The openings of Hopkins' poems, we have seen, are often abrupt intrusions on consciousness that proclaim their difference from the time that preceded the saying: "Thou mastering me / God!" or "No worst, there is none." Not so, his endings. The closures of the poems typically seek to prevent a sharp line of demarcation; many poems seem to want to continue, however impossible that may be, after the sounds cease.[4] So the poem's *process* often echoes or underlies the idea of the poem as loss.

"Pied Beauty," for example, seeks at its end to "Praise him" beyond the limits of the poem, and perhaps beyond the limits of language as well:

> All things counter, original, spare, strange;
>   Whatever is fickle, freckled (who knows how?)
>   With swift, slow; sweet, sour; adazzle, dim;
> He fathers-forth whose beauty is past change:
>   Praise him.

The poem tries to break through the natural constraints of its own medium as the structure forces the reader to prolong the closing words.[5] The concluding clause, "Praise him," is startlingly concise, a forceful summary command, but the clause emerges quietly, the sounds of the words' ends linger, and the poem's structure and meaning lead us to dwell on and in the final words. The reader's impulse is to prolong those two syllables, "Praise him," to protract the sounding of them so that their duration in time matches that of the other lines. Through structure, through meaning, and through sound, Hopkins attempts to sustain the experience of assent, to make it lasting.

That so many poems end in the suggestion of incipient flight prolongs the experience of the poem into the time that succeeds the saying. These endings glimpse and so start the reader toward something "yonder" in both space *and* time. The images of bird and flight suggest all their traditional Romantic connotations, the longed-for freedom from earth's mortal pull, although now, in Hopkins, that freedom is to be used to soar to a specific, directed end. That is, flight in Hopkins enacts the directions of assent. The poem's image begins to soar into seemingly limitless space as it moves out and up toward an immortal future:

> —Where kept? do but tell us where kept, where.—
> Yonder.—What high as that! We follow, now we follow.—
>   Yonder, yes yonder, yonder,
> Yonder.
>
> ("The Golden Echo")

> let joy size
>
> At God knows when to God knows what; whose smile
> 's not wrung, see you; unforeseen times rather—as skies
> Betweenpie mountains—lights a lovely mile.
>
> ("My own heart")

> The heart rears wings bold and bolder
> And hurls for him, O half hurls earth for him off under his
>   feet.
>
> ("Hurrahing in Harvest")

> Because the Holy Ghost over the bent
>   World broods with warm breast and with ah! bright wings.
>
> ("God's Grandeur")

After the hard bidding of the opening, declaiming itself at us, the poems typically end in something soft and melting, gesturing upward and outward in space *and* time as they hint at the yet greater wonder:

> Man's spirit will be flesh-bound when found at best,
>   But uncumberèd: meadow-down is not distressed
>   For a rainbow footing it nor he for his bónes rísen.
>
> ("The Caged Skylark")

Half realization, half anticipation, the endings direct us as the sounds of language fade away. The poet relies on the hush of a final unstressed syllable or on final consonants that linger to suggest that there is more than what has been (or possibly ever can be) articulated:

> The thunder-purple seabeach plumèd purple-of-thunder,
> If a wuthering of his palmy snow-pinions scatter a colossal
>   smile
> Off him, but meaning motion fans fresh our wits with
>   wonder.
>
> ("Henry Purcell")

> For Christ plays in ten thousand places,
> Lovely in limbs, and lovely in eyes not his
> To the Father through the features of men's faces.
>
> ("As kingfishers catch fire")

In such endings, the sounds die, slowly, but the experience, ascending, yearns to continue. The image is flying away, just barely at the edge of sight, lighting "a lovely mile." In their attempts to sustain vision and meaning and to prolong the time of the poem, such endings proclaim the fact of loss in their very resistance to losing.

Even when the poem's end is not beginning to soar, it is often countering loss or possible loss with an openly said and enacted effort to forestall what has to come. The repetitious ending of "Inversnaid" may well be like this; that of "Binsey Poplars" surely is:

> Ten or twelve, only ten or twelve
>   Strokes of havoc únselve
>   The sweet especial scene,
>   Rural scene, a rural scene,
>   Sweet especial rural scene.

The speaker here dwells in a memory of that which no longer exists. His words cherish the memory and try to sustain it by repeating themselves in time. In "Brothers," the closure's repetition would similarly hold on. But here it is the idea of Nature's kindness, the boy's effortless goodness, that wants remembering in days to come:

> Ah Nature, framed in fault,
> There's comfort then, there's salt;
> Nature, bad, base, and blind,
> Dearly thou canst be kind;
> There dearly thén, deárly,
> Dearly thou canst be kind.

These endings dramatize the problem posed in "The Leaden Echo and the Golden Echo," where the speaker explicitly asks how to stop time and hold on to beauty. In all these poems, the pointed repetition of language serves as an external sign of the interior process that tries to prevent loss. In a language elsewhere so motionable and dynamic, the repetition shapes a moment strikingly still—and one which by its very nature is always reminding us that it is doomed to pass.

Hopkins makes us aware of loss in any number of other ways. Although he does not, for instance, use more than an average number of present-tense verb forms, the ones he does use make sharp intrusions into the experience of the poem, again lending the sense of spontaneity that bids. The present-tense verbs make us highly conscious of fleeting time, for they are prominently placed, stressed, and often syntactically uncomplicated by modifiers intervening between them and their subjects. In excitement, the speaker points at himself, says "I walk, I lift up, I lift up heart, eyes"; or he points at the world and says, "Summer ends *now*; *now*, barbarous in beauty, the stooks rise" ("Hurrahing in Harvest," [italics added]). The aim is to say the thing that is, to catapult the reader into the instant, but the instant so abruptly and forcefully immediate inevitably suggests its own transience.

Through the transient immediacy of the experiences recorded, through the self-proclaiming sound patterns that insist that we read "with the ears," Hopkins' poetry is always making us aware of loss. As I. A. Richards was first to point out, Hopkins' poems are *about* loss[6]—loss of humanity, loss of grace, loss of self, beauty, and life. And all loss happens in time, through time, because of time:

> The telling time our task is; time's some part,
> Not all, but we were framed to fail and die—
> One spell and well that one. There, ah thereby
> Is comfort's carol of all or woe's worst smart.
>
> ("To his Watch")

It is not just "Summer ends *now*" but "Summer *ends* now." In the most excited exuberance of experience and language, in the hurrahing of the happiest of poems, the need is sensed to seize the moment and stave off the loss that has to come.

That motion—from joy to fear of loss—happens over and over again. "Have, get, *before* it cloy," the speaker of "Spring" pleads with Christ, "*Before* it cloud . . . and sour with sinning, / Innocent mind and Mayday" (italics added). And in the midst of his whole-hearted joy in the seeming perfection of the bugler's first communion, the speaker abruptly turns in fear: "Let mé though see no more of him, and not disappointment / Those sweet hopes quell. . . ." "On the Portrait of Two Beautiful Young People" is rooted in the same fear, for "beauty's dearest veriest vein is tears." In fact, the sharp intake of breath at youth, beauty, or joy so characteristic of Hopkins is just a short step away from his fear of the loss wrought by time. In this sense, the design or argument that follows the image is there to counter loss and the speaker's fear of loss: If indeed the splendid single image is inevitably transient, says the design, it is but one of many, and the principle will endure.

T. S. Eliot's Magus thought that birth and death "were different" until he saw the birth of Christ ("Journey of the Magi"). The idea stands in sharp contrast to Hopkins' speaker, who is never under any such illusion. For him, the moments of splendor in the natural world are the very moments that enfold both phenomena, the moments of beauty in the unselving, of the gold in the fall—or better, of the gold *of* the fall, a goldenfall. Creation is never far from destruction, nor growth from decay.

Thus, what at first appears a fall may be wholly other; if loss is inevitable in the Heraclitean world, the moment of losing is precious. So Hopkins attends to downward motion—the motion of the bird and the leaf and the river, of the man at work, and of the modest boy who stands at the door while his brother performs on stage. Hopkins must seize the day in its transience: If summer ends now, then this is the time when one may find cause to hurrah in harvest.

"Felix Randal" takes its plot from the paradoxical nature of life: Strong in body, the farrier was yet weak in soul; as his body and mind deteriorate, he gradually achieves a stronger spiritual self (the two vectors cross, a *felix culpa* enacted by the sonnet's form, in the sacrament given by the priest). At the last he joins the strength of his soul with the past strength of his body in the transformation and apotheosis of his death. Yet Hopkins makes the sonnet more complex than the neatness of this represented narrative by grounding the whole poem in the speaker's moving relation to the farrier.

At least in its original form, that relation between the priest and the farrier is born to die:

Felix Randal the farrier, O is he dead then? my duty all ended,

Separated in time and place, the speaker reacts, springs to the news of the farrier's fall. The rhythm, absolutely colloquial here, seems struck from the speaker at the moment he hears the news. Perhaps it is the "then?" that creates the tone most, stalling for time in a poetry that wastes none. The "then?" seems to figure not loss in poetry but loss in life, the life-loss in which we are at a loss for what to say. If the "O" figures a gathering and catching of self, the "then?" diffuses it, trailing off in a question already answered.

The octave tells the farrier's story, a complexly timed and tensed narrative that ends in the speaker's once again identifiably colloquial voice: "Ah well, God rest him all road ever he offended!" This prayer lends the sense of an ending and exists as a half-dismissal, a willed putting aside of the farrier's life. Indeed, with the particulars told, the sonnet turns, the speaker now free to search out the meaning of his experience with the farrier.

Accordingly, the next words formulate an abstract principle, as if to distance and codify the past relationship with the voice of design: "This seeing the sick endears them to us." The farrier is here one of many, one of "them," the basis for a didactic and dogmatic text. But the speaker cannot sustain this distance. The language begins to repeat itself, but it has turned about and in the same words now refers to the speaker himself: "This seeing the sick endears them to us, us too it endears." Perhaps it is the repetition of "endears" that brings even closer, itself endears, the memory of singular tenderness between the two men, for the distanced generalization now wholly gives way:

> This seeing the sick endears them to us, us too it endears.
> My tongue had taught thee comfort, touch had quenched thy
>   tears,
> Thy tears that touched my heart, child, Felix, poor Felix
>   Randal;

The speaker moves into an experience unnamed in the narrative octave. He moves into a past intimacy, an I/thou encounter that cherishes the singular, individual man when Felix is seen to have touched and to be yet touching the heart of the priest. The speaker's admission of love comes closest here, when the only distance left is embodied in the past tense of the verb. With the signal event of this intimacy spoken, the third line trails off, now in falling rhythms, repeatedly naming the man. This tender naming of Felix tries to hold on to the experience and to the man; it wants not to relinquish either the remembered intimacy or the remembrance of intimacy. The speaker tries to dwell within this intimacy recreated, newly created, the names stroking the memory and unwilling to release the memory or the man. But the language admits the difficulties of the desire to prolong that intimacy. It admits the difficulties through its falling rhythms, through its repeated pauses, and through the slowing of enacted time that comes with the repeated naming—"child, Felix, poor Felix Randal."

In extended exclamation, the last three lines shake the poem back into narrative movement, directing the experience of loss in the world and in the poem:

How far from then forethought of, all thy more boisterous
  years,
When thou at the random grim forge, powerful amidst peers,
Didst fettle for the great grey drayhorse his bright and
  battering sandal!

In their willful confusion of time sense, the lines would have us
see an unforeseen persistence through time, a newly found inti-
mation of immortality. The lines move back into chronological
time in order to soar forth into a future that escapes time. The
named, remembered, and 'visible' past, the physical image, turns
symbol; the Christian escape, triumphant, embodied in the repre-
sentational image of the farrier's early work, is now joyously cele-
brated by a speaker whom it leaves behind. As always, not intimate
human relationships inevitably subject to decay but the symbol,
which spans time, spells the future. The glimmer of flight is there,
the mythological flying steed in the "bright and battering sandal,"
and that image gleaned from the far past now directs and deter-
mines the future.

The closing image of the farrier forging that sandal tells us of
past intimations of immortality at the same time that it is detailing
a concrete past long gone. While saying his human joy, Hopkins
is again reminding us of its transience. Human life, even at its
fullest, perhaps most when at its fullest, is inexorably subject to
loss. Countering the endless human loss comes only Christ's design,
which allows duration and endurance, and which turns loss into a
hint of final gain in a time beyond human time.

The finding of Felix Randal's powerful direction toward heaven
within an image of what had seemed an undirected life is a finding
of recurrence, the only holding possible in a Christian, linear on-
tology. Exact repetition of event and being are possible only within
a primitive, cyclical world view where "through . . . repetition,
time is suspended, or at least its virulence is diminished."[7] Chris-
tianity restores time and progress because the original fall, the
coming, and the second coming are singular events—the only truly
singular events—and so create discernible time. They give direction

and force to Christian time; they give history meaning. All the stress felt by man, writes Hopkins, "dates from day / Of his going in Galilee" (*Deutschland*, 7).[8] Because it ceases to be random, time within the Christian world is irreversible, irreplaceable, and unrepeatable. Thus, in the Christian world view, exact repetition of consciousness or happening is impossible.[9] Man is trapped within the fact of his mortality, and "After-comers cannot guess the beauty been" ("Binsey Poplars").

In an undergraduate essay, Hopkins defines beauty as a tension between sameness and difference, and uses the device of rhyme to illustrate and epitomize the principle.[10] As J. Hillis Miller has indicated, all of Hopkins' poems exist as a tour de force of rhyme, rhyming words, phrases, ideas, and things as well as sounds.[11] Implicitly, rhyming is omnipresent in Hopkins because "Christ plays in ten thousand places"—because what is fathered forth rhymes with the fatherer.

Recurrence is the rhyming—the sameness with difference—that happens in time. It partially compensates for inevitable loss in that it partially stays time in its looking backward, in its overt connection or rhyming of human experience. The event of Christ's coming gives direction to history and in so doing creates the possibility of symbol in the world: Inherent in every physical event is its representational, recurrent meaning. Iconographically, Hopkins captures and recaptures that coming and so recovers meaning for otherwise disconnected events. If the *haecceitas* of every being is inescapable, recurrence constitutes a kind of earthly salvation, a continuity of grace and purpose in worldly time.

Furthermore, Hopkins seems always to be confirming or validating the thematic recurrence he speaks of by what is happening in his language. The motionable, chiming language enacts a poetic recurrence for the speaker and reader in their experience of time in saying the poem. Hopkins is hardly alone in using mimetic, suggestive sound and rhythm, but the degree to which he makes us aware of them, stresses them, is unusual. It is largely because of its recurrent sounds that his language seems meant to be read aloud. And read aloud, the poetry proclaims the principle of recurrence all the more strongly, making us know the sameness-with-difference as a dramatic experience in sounded time as well as on the space of the page. Theme is made process again, the dogma turned into a way of seeing.

When, in "The Blessed Virgin compared to the Air we Breathe," the speaker finds the sound of the word "air" in "Mary," he is finding linguistic recurrence that would confirm principle in the world. Indeed, the speaker frequently appears to confirm thought with language—as if sounds closely related to one another were there to convince us that the things and events they name are closely related:[12]

As *k*ing*f*ishers *c*atch *f*ire, *dr*agon*f*lies *dr*aw *f*lame;

Each animal's name contains, at the beginning of a stressed syllable, a sound that recurs at the beginning of its verb or action, and another that recurs at the beginning of the verb's direct object. Each animal, then, is closely identified with what it does. But the analogy between the two actions is also stressed by recurring rhythm:

kíng	físh	ērs	cátch	fíre
drág	ōn	flíes	dráw	fláme

The spondees draw the weight of the line's stress into the beings' actions (where Hopkins obviously wants it), but they also make known a second rhythmical configuration that is strongly analogous to—but not exactly like—the first. The rhyming of the two actions in the space of the world becomes a recurrence in sounded time for the reader.

The force of boldly recurrent sound and rhythm is felt repeatedly, in all of Hopkins; the speaking voice is always experiencing in the event of the poem a recurrence not unlike what the speaker is reporting in the world. "Now burn, new born to the world, / Double-naturèd name" (*Deutschland*, 34), the speaker implores Christ, and the reader may be the more ready to assent to the "Double-naturèd name" because of the previous doubling in sound and rhythm: "Now burn, new born."

Similarly, the end of "That Nature is a Heraclitean Fire" leads us to assent to the seemingly impossible recurrence it names by the way it apprehends the idea:

In a flash, at a trumpet crash,
I am all at once what Christ is, ' since he was what I am, and
This Jack, joke, poor potsherd, ' patch, matchwood, immortal
    diamond,
               Is immortal diamond.

In the next to last line, all of time is collapsed into the two 'time-less' focal points of Christian time. In the speed of the rhythms and monosyllabic words—a speed suggestive of the instantaneous transformation—the first verses strain against the temporal na-ture of their own medium. The verbs "am . . . is . . . was . . . am . . . / . . . Is" mirror the reciprocity of the two moments, the rhymed interchange, in an explanation of absolute simplicity. Christ's mortal existence ("he was") is at the center, making the whole recurrence possible.

In the last line, the accumulation of stressed, rhymed things that together spell man results in the reader's increasing attention to the ungainly, recurring sounds. The "immortal diamond" at the end of this swollen line is almost lost in the long list of trivial objects and demeaning names that precedes it. Thus the poem's last words, direct repetition on the page, intend and achieve a stunning surprise. The reader accepts, assents to, and trusts this 'shock' because of its antecedent. In the verbal repetition, the full import of what was there before flashes out into meaning. When the concealed diamond emerges, Hopkins succeeds in rhyming per-fection, immortality, and transcendent beauty—"in a flash"—with the very mankind that the poem had almost despaired of. Here, the fact of the recurrence *is* the meaning, and the stunning repe-tition on the page would stop man for all time.

The pattern is familiar. In Hopkins, although it may at first appear to come from nowhere, the revelation always emerges from obscurity, from where it was hiding. In retrospect, we see it anew, now recognizing the anticipatory hint, the seed or symbol, for what it always was. It is in fact the continuity of recurrence that makes design or abstraction existent and intelligible. Good or bad, good and bad, "From life's dawn it is drawn down" (*Deutschland*, 20). And we return in order to know the place for the first time: "Over again I feel thy finger and find thee" (*Deutschland*, 1).

Always assenting to something anterior, something that was once a presence, recurrence locates its own present in relation to another time and space, sound and place. So, in affirming the past, recurrence attempts to store a self, a sighting, and thus deny a fearful fragmentation. If exact repetition is impossible in this world view, so too is absolute isolation, the still death. While recurrence points backward to resay a saying, it also points to itself in its saying that this is *not* the same, for it is another saying, and now is not then. That which is new in recurrent experience validates difference, selfhood, and change; it mocks the dying of the light. Exact repetition, were it possible, would annihilate time and difference; recurrence creates the vitality and intensity of the felt continuous.

In two poems especially—"Felix Randal" and "Spring and Fall"— the explicit subject of recurrence and even the recurrence of sound and language pales before the experience of a speaker who dramatically reenacts recurrence. The speaker of "Felix Randal," perhaps against his own expectations, brings the past to life, which allows a kind of redemption to happen in the poem; the speaker of "Spring and Fall" undergoes an experience in the poem that, in its affirmation of recurrence, contradicts or at the least profoundly tempers the sense of the design.

We return to "Felix Randal," where not only do ideas and language recur, but recurrence itself becomes a temporal experience for the speaker as he speaks.[13] The poem is a study of loss and gain through interior mental and emotional processes that turn loss into continuing presence. We know, first of all, the chronological time of the speaker's speaking, and this ongoing chronological time of the speaker plays against other experiential times that are discovered within the self or are created by the drama of the poem. These fuller experiences of time are realized and become dominant as they emerge out of and counter the speaker's chronological time. Chronological time thus informed by the speaker's inner experience is instressed, and it is this compounding of time senses which creates experiential time and meaning for the speaker; it makes possible unforeseen discovery in the poem as it reenacts intrinsic revelatory and redemptive design in the world.

The poem begins with loss and gain—gain because Felix Randal comes into the speaker's mind so markedly after an absence unthought of, loss because the news of his death makes the farrier's absence present. The paradox goes further as the poem becomes a testing of whether that absence, death, is a real absence. The knowledge of Felix Randal's death fills the speaker's consciousness, starts it on a quest toward assent as he tries to fill the absence with a past made present through memory. The poem, in fact, lives the past over twice, once in the octave and once in the sestet. And these retrograde motions of retrospection play against the continuing, ongoing linear dimensions of the speaker speaking.

At the same time, there is not only the farrier's absence, which must be filled within the speaker, but an absence in the speaker himself. The two are yoked together, each pulling the other toward assent and ascent: "O is he dead then? my duty all ended . . . ?" The quest to make good the absence of Felix is also a quest to make good an absence of self.

The octave is largely a narrative of memory, of linear time within the present, ongoing time of the speaker speaking. Here, memory rediscovers the farrier, but only barely. Although the voice approaches a lyrical dimension in its physical description of Felix, the octave is essentially a recitation and not an evocation:

> Felix Randal the farrier, O is he dead then? my duty all
>   ended,
> Who have watched his mould of man, big-boned and hardy-
>   handsome
> Pining, pining, till time when reason rambled in it and some
> Fatal four disorders, fleshed there, all contended?
>
> Sickness broke him. Impatient, he cursed at first, but mended
> Being anointed and all; though a heavenlier heart began some
> Months earlier, since I had our sweet reprieve and ransom
> Tendered to him. Ah well, God rest him all road ever he
>   offended!

The linear sequence of the processes of retrospection is similar to the linear sequence of the speaker's speaking. But simultaneously, for all its sameness, the voiced experience of retrospection begins to mount from the speaker's speech as if it might overcome that ongoing voice and veer beyond clear chronicle toward empathy, as in the very recurring sounds and words of "Pining, pining, till time when reason rambled." Later, the clear chronology is shaken again when the speaker qualifies his statement of fact and, in so doing, doubles back to reconsider and expand on the summary already offered: "though a heavenlier heart began some / Months earlier." The drama of the voices of time begins to reconstitute the presence of both Felix and the speaker, and hints at a more real fullness of time and experience to come.

The narrative octave of memory, then, partially recovers the physical image, recalls the strength of Felix, but moves on to the loss of that strength and the priest's blessing, a blessing that occurs both in the past and now in the present moment at the edge of memory: "Ah well, God rest him all road ever he offended!" With that, the poem seems to return to the single dimension of the chronological time of the speaker speaking. The blessing offers an easy assumption of ending, of memory returning to the present tense. Yet the return distances the speaker from Felix and himself, the immediate present holding a greater absence because of the failure to make either the self or Felix, glimpsed in the octave, a real and sustained presence. The blessing as blessing is formulaic, yet the slight distortion of syntax may suggest a slight hesitation within the self rather than a complete resolution.

Memory does return in the sestet but not to narrative recitation and sequentiality. Rather, after a momentary deflection, it returns to a lyricism that immerses itself in a moment of experience and dwells in that experience:

This seeing the sick endears them to us, us too it endears.
My tongue had taught thee comfort, touch had quenched thy
    tears,
Thy tears that touched my heart, child, Felix, poor Felix
    Randal;

Chronology is lost, and the loss is gain. The momentary deflection, the generalization on the text of the first half of the first line, bends back into the self as the speaker realizes his own gain in ministering to Felix. The past empathy between the speaker and Felix recurs then, is made both present and presence—compounded because existing both now and then. It is the same empathy yet different and multiple because, more than empathy in memory recounted, it is held in slow time, reflected upon and reflecting back: "endears . . . us, /us . . . endears"; "child, Felix, poor Felix Randal."

Duty then is not ended. As Felix and the speaker "touch" one another, all the doublings touch and converge, flowing into assent:

How far from then forethought of, all thy more boisterous
        years,
When thou at the random grim forge, powerful amidst peers,
Didst fettle for the great grey drayhorse his bright and
        battering sandal!

Assenting to the touch and because touched, the speaker in the final tercet moves deeply into a now more deeply known past. The motion is an assent to the intimacy reknown. The self once known is no longer absent. Nor is Felix. Although the farrier's power is presented once more, it is no longer physical power but metaphorical power. The past has become a continuously active presence, the imaged flight of the "battering sandal." Touched by "touch" and "tears," the self merges into the real river of time and, as it emerges in one of its recurrent surfacings, overtakes and suspends the chronological voice of the speaker. The speaker's final motion into the past becomes his assent as well as a mode of rising to what has now been revealed as a previously unseen, unknown, unforethought of assent and ascension.

It is, ironically, the poet who has gained for the priest what the priest had lost. And it is in all senses the poet who realizes the gain. The poet's ministering rediscovers through the recurring dramas of the speaker in the poem the recurring dramas of redemptive presence. And this is not, as is more usual in Hopkins, gleaned from without, from the world, but from within—not from the Holy Ghost coming in revelation as the morning emerges from the obscurity of darkness, nor even the direct assent of the heart in hiding, stirring outward in instinctual response. But with greater difficulty and through labyrinthine currents of the interior made real, made felt, by language as sign of that interior, the hiding and shifting centers of recurrent experience emerge to displace chronological time and to speak of, and in speaking fill, a continuous presence.

More consciously, more directly than "Felix Randal," "Spring and Fall" reaches into the past to find a future. It reaches back to origins—to our origins and to its own origins, to the ontological and epistemological sources of being—to find recurrence through time. Uncharacteristically for Hopkins, the poem names no ultimate redemption. It leaves us instead with pathos, with a saying of human loss in life and of death as the mortal direction of all. At the same time, the speaker's temporal experience in the poem would gainsay that pathos and find a more human and hopeful event. As in "Felix Randal," in "Spring and Fall," the speaker's experience of recurrence revises the explicit saying of the poem.

"Spring and Fall" is motivated by Hopkins' characteristic 'Why?'—the question which precedes the finding of an anterior, the 'before' and 'behind' of phenomena. Perhaps the poem is able to go as far as it does toward that anterior because it discovers location and definition of what is anterior in visible time and space—the child, Margaret, who sits in front of and outside the speaker. The speaker implicitly modifies the didactic 'answers' he finds by grounding them in the moving relationship between himself and the child. That is, the poem formulates with clarity the answers to the questions it raises, yet as in "Felix Randal," the experience of the poem resides just as strongly in the more problematic and complex motions of the speaker toward the other person. (It is not just "Spring and Fall" but "Spring and Fall: to a young child.") As age reaches back to its origin in youth, the motion of the speaker toward the child itself finds a source, a spring of being, within the poem.

Faced with her first experience of fall, Margaret reacts in a way that the speaker cannot. Thus the poem's rhetorical situation dramatizes from the start the blight that man was born for: For the first time the young child sees the unleaving of life, and she weeps; the older man sees it for the thousandth time, and he speaks.

The speaker's words seek out the child's response and, in so doing, seek out a beginning of time in which words themselves were unnatural:

> Márgarét, áre you gríeving
> Over Goldengrove unleaving?

The leaves fall down, the leaves fall down and die. Margaret's tears fall down *over* (in space and 'because of') the leaves; her tears, too, will die. The rhyming begins as both the leaves and the child appear to advantage in their falling. The leaves are golden—beautiful, valuable, rare—at the moment when they unselve, fall, and die. But "unleaving" also suggests 'not leaving'—staying, lasting, permanency.[14] And 'golden' also suggests long-lastingness or timelessness. Thus, the speaker's words intimate the original "Goldengrove unleaving," the "Eden garden" ("Spring") that haunts mankind by its absence, and the poem widens to carry the implications of the original fall of man as well as the immediate and recurrent one. The first fall, original, causes all the others.

The second question is a revision of the first, the tone of wonder growing even as it is defined:

> Leáves, líke the things of man, you
> With your fresh thoughts care for, can you?

The simplicity and directness of the first couplet have yielded to a more complex syntax, an order of thought disjuncted and difficult. In their repetition and rhyming, the 'you's are stressed, in effect repeating the meaning of the syntax and further differentiating the child from the speaker.

"Leaves" are foliage, of course, but by now they must also be 'leave-takings'—which *are* the "things of man." Margaret, her fresh thoughts undissociated from emotion, can care. The speaker sounds affectionate, bemused, fatherly, and already aware of his own loss of fresh thoughts, of care, in marking his separation from the child. Yet if the syntax is fragmented, disjuncted, and intellected, and if it so marks a separation from the lack of similarity to the child, Hopkins' sense units betray a rhyming of motion and rhythm:

Léaves | líke thē thíngs | of mán
yóu | Wīth your frésh | thoúghts cáre

That is, the child's weeping makes the speaker aware of another 'leave-taking'—her tears evoke an awareness of his own lack of tears—yet at the same time, his own phrases subtly rhyme. The springs of a sympathetic remembrance of feeling stir even as he suggests that, for him, they will no longer flow.

In the lack of rhyming between Margaret and himself, the speaker finds his transition:

Áh! ás the heart grows older
It will come to such sights colder
By and by, nor spare a sigh
Though worlds of wanwood leafmeal lie;

As she approaches her own winter in age, Margaret, the speaker says, will be sighless and sightless, colder and uncaring. The speaker's "By and by" with its echo of resigned leave-taking ('bye and bye') posits time, careless time, as well as space, removed space, all in contrast to Margaret's present weeping "over" the fallen leaves.

The speaker seems to be growing older in front of us. His statement explaining the difference between youth and age, child and self, is didactic, an apparent retreat from earlier sympathy. But his tone is quiet, almost meditational, and the lines in their motion betray more of the speaker than the speaker himself seems aware of.

We have seen the leaves turn out to *be* the things of man (instead of being analogous to or "líke" them). "Such sights" works in the same way: In her rhyming with the leaves, Margaret herself is such a sight. That is, the speaker's larger point of view sees Margaret as well as the leaves in the flowering of the fall, in the flowering that *is* the fall. Her tears spring and fall, and in her weeping Margaret 'leaves' with the leaves. Her expression of innocence is inevitably a loss of innocence; she is, all unknown to her, moving closer toward the speaker. Meanwhile, the speaker is saying that age cannot react so sympathetically to "such sights," but the poem rebukes the whole idea, and nowhere does it do so more than in these lines.

For "such sights" is not the only indistinction of statement here. The "Áh!"—that open syllable held, the exclaimed interjection so characteristic of Hopkins—seems born for this poem, this place. In that open syllable held, the highly articulated consciousness that speaks the poem retreats to let the speaker breathe out, just once, all that his verbal awareness would guard against. And it is as if the suspension of "Áh!" does not want to end, as if the speaker would dwell there if he could, wanting not to be born out of that sympathy breathed, nor borne forward from it. In the "Áh!" Margaret's tears find the form of sound in the speaker, his exclamation barely escaping the self even as it discovers a self that the speaker does not wholly recognize. An instinctive exclamation of pity for the future unweeping Margaret and for the speaker himself who is supposed to be like the future unweeping Margaret he projects, the "Áh!" arrests the poem. The lines speak of a future disconnection, speak to a failure of recurrence, but as that syllable is held in its slow falling, it catches and reenacts the bright wings: The "Áh!" *is* recurrence because the "Áh!" subsiding and ascending at once is the *speaker's* spring and fall. The syllable responds emotionally to the imaginative connection made, and it so belies by its very existence the statement that the grown cannot spare a sigh. It *is* a sigh—if only a sigh—and it so spells his—and Margaret's—salvation. The child's sympathy is not wholly lost in the man. (And having said that, one begins to wonder if that disembodied world, that "wanwood leafmeal," does not "lie" in another sense— the leaves lie, perhaps, because to the voice behind the speaker's voice the afterlife exists.)

The next line, a structural surprise, forms a triplet at the center of the poem:

> And yet you *will* weep and know why.

The verse pulls the speaker out of himself and back into the world, out of the hypothetical future and back into the present falling. In effect, the line returns the poem "to a young child." It is not enough, the speaker consciously realizes, to tell the child that her sorrow will pass. "*Will*" may be future tense, but as I. A. Richards first pointed out,[15] the line may also be read as the emphatic present: 'And yet you insist in weeping and on knowing why.' Since Hopkins italicized the "*will*," the second reading may well be the intended one. Even so, the line remains ambiguously simple, gathering up all human seeking after the cause for suffering.

All the sadness in the world comes together as the poem's implications widen:

> Now no matter, child, the name:
> Sórrow's spríngs áre the same.

The word, the name—like her name here—does not matter because the emotion and the fact do matter now. Sorrow springs from the blight man was born for, from his dying, from the dying of his heart. But the poem does not name this cause yet. The second line in particular achieves a simplicity and even sureness in its syntax, sound, and meaning, all of which seem to be leading toward the answer named, the explanation given.

Once again, however, the explanation is forestalled, and the poem is momentarily deflected:

> Nor mouth had, no nor mind, expressed
> What heart heard of, ghost guessed:

The expressions of age, we are told, cannot begin to approximate the intuitive responses of the soul, the springs of feeling. The spirited rumors of mystery and emotion are uncatchable in language or conscious thought. After the child-directed simplicity of the previous statement, these lines move back to complex abstraction. The syntax is as contorted as any in the entire poem, and the verses again work at a level of intellect the child could not understand. It is as if the speaker has stepped back, fearful of seeming to say it all, fearful of the simplicity of the word he has come upon.

But again, even here, we catch the echoes come from a farther room. If the syntax is mature, the meaning harks back to the remembrance of youth. To reaffirm, as these lines do, the primacy of that mysterious heart sympathy, the speaker has had to have felt that sympathy and must now remember—under the child's tutelage—something of what that experience was. The very contortion of the language seems a willed defense against the experience, the heart's hearing. The didacticism of these lines, the disjunction they say so absolutely, is yet open to question because those rhyme words—"expressed" and "guessed" (also heard as 'guest')—do come together in rhyme.

At the end the speaker returns to "sorrow's springs" to answer grandiloquently all the questions asked:

It ís the blight man was born for,

Man was born for blight—sickness, devastation, disease, the failure of the human crop, the fall of worlds, the fall of man. All of this, Margaret mourns in its inescapable recurrence. But "It" in this line must also refer to the previous couplet: "It" is also that man cannot make his words mean what he wants them to, cannot fit words to feeling, logic to emotion, sense to mystery; that as he grows greater in word power, he grows increasingly impotent in the power of his feelings to respond.

And the speaker's words have grown great indeed. "It ís the blight man was born for" tolls down at its audience, all impressive and all-encompassing. The tragic didacticism sounds good, but it is all futile to alleviate, console, or perhaps even to explain Margaret's weeping to man or child. As impressive as these words sound, they exist almost completely as sign, as object, as the hardest otherness and the one farthest from Margaret's tears. They are in sharp contrast to the "Áh!," that unformulated word, all indistinction, that bends the sign back into the self. "It ís the blight man was born for" is almost pure sign, the harsh motion of unforgiving otherness.

At the very end, the speaker's thought 'buckles,' plunging from that encompassing universal to the individual child:

It is Margaret you mourn for.

Her name does matter, and it matters because his words fall from his own recurring spring. Like leaves, like the things of man, his words must fall and fail; and yet they have sprung from a source that thought had lost, beyond saving and caring, and even in their falling are hardly guessed at. The harshness, the hardness of pronouncement, is tempered by the humanness. Margaret mourns her spring, which is her fall. Her dawn, her morning, her spring, intimates her even-ing, her fall, her death. They are all one, and they are all subject to that blight: the spring, the fall, Margaret, the wood, mankind. That this, the last line, glances back to gather in the previous line and temper that hardness and show it all one is evident in the interchangeable homonyms of the rhyme words— "born" may be heard as 'borne,' and "mourn" as 'morn.' The verses would so exchange meanings, yet the couplet's meaning would remain the same. The phenomena are one, the child's springing the same as her falling.

Thus, the closure of the poem is as complete in rhyme as in rhythm as in sense; poetic closure is, in fact, as complete as is imaginable, and the end is memorable. The end affects us because of the strength of the closure; because of the strength of "blight" and "Margaret" within the simplicity of the diction and sense; and because, most of all, of what happens between the two lines, the connective fall enacted, the forgiveness arrived at. Yet this revision, as powerful and as memorable as it is, affirms some of the separation of man and child spoken of. The child cries in assent to the sadness; the man's words assent to the fact that the world has to be so; that it has to be so posits the acceptance of the hardness of age, assents in spite of its sense to the loss of sympathy in age. For all its mercy, for all its human-directed tenderness, "It is Margaret you mourn for" yet looks down at the child, consciously bending the sign and the voice saying it toward the object, the other.

It is much earlier, in the "Áh!" that the speaker *is* the child, re-enacting the child's act, which is itself an age-old recurrence. The poem centers and lives in its dying, springs in its own fall. The ripeness is all: the grove golden and dying, the child's tears, and the "Áh!" breathed in empathy for the child, for the self, and for the unselving of both. The child responds to the unselving of trees, the speaker responds to the unselving of child, the reader responds to the unselving of speaker. And all responses in their springing forth may at the same time reach back to re-enact and re-sound the original and recurring unselving of self.

V

Recurrences: *The Wreck of the Deutschland*

The Wreck of the Deutschland is the first of Hopkins' mature poems and the poem that broke his years of poetic silence. Far longer and more complex than anything that Hopkins was ever again to achieve in poetry, *The Wreck of the Deutschland* is a kind of center and circumference of the poet's work, a most "subtle and recondite" shaping of energies through time.[1] If the poem is exceptional among the mature poems for its length and scope, it finds its impulse differently too. *The Wreck of the Deutschland* is occasional, celebrating a specific historical event in the world. Yet Hopkins pulls this more public purpose inward and anticipates the intimacy of his later lyrics while relinquishing none of the shipwreck's more embracing implications. He entwines the larger event into the speaker's past and present experience. Thus, *The Wreck of the Deutschland* retells climactic events in the lives of the nun and of the speaker, but it also makes recurrent drama of the speaker's experience with language in the poem.

The occasion was Hopkins' starting point; his task, not the making of order out of event but rather, as always, the finding or discovery of order in the event. Hopkins writes to his mother that the disaster "made a deep impression on me, more than any other wreck or accident I ever read of."[2] The very violence of the signal happening seems to attract him, compelling interpretation. In Hopkins, not the least of God's reasons for violence is that violence forces man's attention, intensifies his awareness, and may direct that keen awareness to something beyond the self. The poem's responsibility is to decipher the sign—to read the meaning there to be read. The poem is concerned not only with reading particular signs but with establishing the crucial importance of reading signs:

> But wé dream we are rooted in earth—Dust!
> Flesh falls within sight of us, we, though our flower the
> same,
> Wave with the meadow, forget that there must
> The sour scythe cringe, and the blear share come.   (*11*)

Even the most obvious sign, the most recurring sign, we forget to read, and the consequences, the speaker implies, are tragic. These lines occur at the start of the poem's second part; thus, Hopkins, with his "passion for explanation," sets out to 'read' the sign of the wreck of the Deutschland.

The poem sets out, then, to do no less than explain the reason for catastrophe in the world, to understand how a merciful God can be—and is—also a mastering and violent one. The conception of the poem is inextricably bound up with Christian paradox, and Hopkins mines both Old and New Testaments to do his reading or exegesis of the event. But as in later poems, the speaker integrates the biblical allusions into his ongoing vision of the existing world—the readings have to be rediscovered in the here and now in order to have meaning and validity.[3] The reader perceives the allusions not as extrinsically imposed on the poem but intrinsically found in the world, visible anew.

Hopkins, we know, began composing the poem—began writing poetry after years without serious poetic endeavor—with the straightforward narrative which now appears in stanza twelve: "On Saturday sailed from Bremen, / American-outward-bound. . . ."[4] That is, he started to write at the beginning of the story or 'plot' of the focal event; he strove to retell the event clearly, to establish the reading on the text as given. But he then put that text aside and turned to revise it with what is now Part the First, the story of the speaker's own wreck—his own past turning and saying of yes.

The finished poem incorporates the retelling of two separate events, each one having emerged under the pressure of God's violent mastery. The poem moves from the first event, the speaker's confession in terror, his saying of yes, to the second event, a saying of yes within the physical terror, the surrounding pressure of the death-dealing storm, and so implies by the conjunction an analogy through time, a recurrence.[5] That is, the speaker sees his own mastering through the later and larger event, the wreck of the Deutschland: His turning becomes a type of the nun's. (Because of the poem's ordering, the reader reverses the events' relation and sees the nun's event in light of the speaker's.) Still, this is not yet enough: At the end, both events yield to the further vision, the speaker's hope that within the second text, the nun's assent, there was that which would provoke or signal the still larger turning and assent, the "shipwreck" turned "harvest," the conversion of all England to Catholicism:[6]

> Dame, at our door
> Drowned, and among our shoals,
> Remember us in the roads, the heaven-haven of the
> reward:
> Our King back, Oh, upon English souls!
> Let him easter in us, be a dayspring to the dimness of us,
> be a crimson-cresseted east,
> More brightening her, rare-dear Britain, as his reign rolls, (35)

In later life, the movement forward becomes characteristic of the work of Hopkins, who is always looking for the "river" that "rides time," Christ's life turned into the current that gives meaningful direction to time. Just as Hopkins is not satisfied to stay within the discrete and personal self, he is not satisfied to stay within the discrete moment, no matter how it holds his attention or how full it is. Both moment or event and self must be seen in relation to, and thus as recurrences of, a larger perspective; for Hopkins that larger perspective is the line of Christian history.

As often with Hopkins, the Romantic ontology sets his pattern into strong relief. In "Kubla Khan," an archetype of Romantic poems, Coleridge grasps the single moment, a moment of overwhelming plenitude, and with it displaces all others. The poem represents the single idiosyncratic event, the event that dominates and even obliterates recurrence and time. Indeed, the poem's vision was so much a part of its moment, we are told, that when the moment had passed, Coleridge could not return to the poem—the vision would not recur.

Of course for Hopkins no such moment is imaginable if for no other reason than because Christ will not allow such displacement of his thrust and significance. So Margaret's tears must be seen as loss through time, and every loss through time, as the very "blight man was born for." But the mind which wants to turn the particular event into symbol is not only Christian; it is also Victorian.

The Victorian self is dependent, at times even overcome by forces uncontrolled and uncontrollable. Characteristically the Victorian entwines the self and its moment into a larger perspective, a perspective defined variously but consistently needing to place the self within a larger context and understand the self within larger forces in time. Arnold is an obvious example: The historical places and monuments in his poems are public and accessible avenues to an external context of cultural myth through time; more integrally, the signal elm tree in "Thyrsis," the fact that it still stands, that the light still gleams, and that the Scholar-Gipsy still roams, are all signs of the larger recurrence upon which the personal self relies for identity through time. In Arnold, the lasting of the self rests upon the lasting of the symbol. And while Arnold finds his context in a myth of culture, Carlyle turns to the recurrence of great men. Although Carlyle's heroes logically extend the Byronic cult of the individual, Carlyle puts that Romantic hero to Victorian use: The hero becomes a model for right behavior, and the reader is urged to follow, to copy, the hero—to make of him a pattern of recurrence who does not leap up from the race of common men.

In his turn, each of the Victorians seems to find his own historical vehicle. In *The Idylls of the King*, Tennyson grasps literary myth, finding in the nobility of the doomed Round Table the analogue and validation of the Victorian enterprise. The Oxford movement itself may express the need for a larger context: the history of the institutionalized, orthodox Roman Church. Marx posits economics as the determinant of history, and Darwin reaches back further than anyone to piece together a scientific myth of the history of life itself. Common to all these historical conceptions is that the self is seen as symptomatic rather than idiosyncratic or exceptional, the overview gathering both personal self and discrete event into the embracing myth. It is as if the idylls of the past existed in large part to secure, authenticate, and even constitute the Victorian sense of self.

In Hopkins, the self must constitute itself within the momentum of Christian history moving toward its right end. The speaker of the *Deutschland* finds the explanation of his personal past and even of his entire being within the historical past of Christ's life, from which the self arises. There is no doubt in the speaker's clear formulation: "It dates from day / Of his going in Galilee" (7). "It" here represents the stress and stroke experienced by the speaker in his conversion but also that felt later by "Two hundred souls in the round" (12), among them the nun who responds, and finally the stress and stroke of all life, past, passing, and to come. Christ's "going" is the singular event in time; the God who sends Christ is "Ground of being, and granite of it" (32). Christ's life provides the context for all life: "it rides time like riding a river" (6); God is "a sovereignty that heeds but hides, bodes but abides" (32), "With a mercy that outrides / The all of water" (33).

Thus, the stories of nun and self. But had Hopkins stopped there, he would have left a poem confident in its own didacticism. Instead—and this makes all the difference—the speaker, sure that the answers he seeks are there, embedded in the extrinsic world, shares his uncertainties of reading, the *process* of finding order, and so enacts a second drama in the poem. The poem grasps its own false starts, questions the nun's event from a multiplicity of viewpoints (including the historical—see stanza twenty), and records much of its own search for discovery. The process embodied is a dramatic response to fortuitous event; and response to fortuitous event—the event 'signed' by providence—is the theme that gathers up the past quest of the self and of the nun. In the end, the poem itself may be seen as fortuitous event, for there is some conflict between the claims that the poem is making as statement

147

and the claims it is making as poem. The poem says it is reading
signs, says it is exegetical, but the process of the poem strongly
suggests in its ongoing struggle with language that not only is it
reading signs but it is itself a process of creating them.

The nun and the speaker seek the right vein with varying degrees
of difficulty and stress. It is the nun of course who leaps directly
to the mark, and so it is she, the 'other,' who can be most fully
celebrated—another instance of the diminishment or dependency
of the self. (In this sense, the poem is "Spring and Fall" all over
again, for the speaker attempts to understand and so repeat the
selving of the character he observes and yet at the same time is
thwarted, locked in his own mortal coil.) The recurrences between
his personal past and the nun's experiences are stressed—but
so, too, are the differences stressed. For the nun, whatever the
meaning of her cry, is stopped within time, her struggle ended
at the instant of her turning. In contrast, the speaker lives on,
continues to be tried, going on beyond both assents, resting "un-
der a roof," "away in the loveable west" (24). That is, by sharp
juxtaposition, Hopkins makes explicit the contrast between the
speaker safe and warm, sheltered and at rest, and the nun, the
"prey of the gales" (24).

But also stressed within the language are the differences between
the speaker's ongoing struggle with language and the nun's direct
finding of the word. The poet phrases the nun's achievement spe-
cifically in terms of her discovery of right language, a discovery
yielded by her right reading of the world and word:

> Ah! there was a heart right!
> There was single eye!
> Read the unshapeable shock night
> And knew the who and the why;
> Wording it how but by him that present and past,
> Heaven and earth are word of, worded by?—   (29)

> For so conceivèd, so to conceive thee is done;
> But here was heart-throe, birth of a brain,
> Word, that heard and kept thee and uttered thee outright. (30)

In the speaker's eye, the nun's word is language wholly unlike his own; it is language not subordinate to life, essential language that engenders Christ and life.[7] Although definable, the nun's word breaks forth beneath the stress and stroke of time; the nun's word is the discrete word that may have been actually charged by the universal.

Moreover, the word that the nun finds in her distress reads not only the storm but the Revelation of Christ. Three times in the last chapter of the last book of the Bible, Christ promises to come again, saying, "I come quickly"; these are, in fact, the last words in the Bible. The nun's cry is a powerful recurrence of the words of the biblical promise. " 'O Christ, Christ, come quickly' " (24) is the biblical word found again, more urgent now in the imperative. The nun manages to make the last word of the Bible her own last word but at the same time a word which is not last but first. For her—and, the speaker hopes, for England—the word is "birth," conception, beginning. Uttering Christ "outright" (30) through a "heart right"—with those words carrying all the directional force of "right" found elsewhere in Hopkins—she gains Christ "for the pain" (31). The suggestion is that the word the nun finds may not be recurrence at all but an absolute and miraculous singularity.[8]

But all pain does not necessarily imply Christ. Finding the right vein may depend upon being immersed in the right chaos:

> One stirred from the rigging to save
> The wild woman-kind below,
> With a rope's end round the man, handy and brave—
> He was pitched to his death at a blow,
> For all his dreadnought breast and braids of thew:
> They could tell him for hours, dandled the to and fro
> Through the cobbled foam-fleece. What could he do
> With the burl of the fountains of air, buck and the flood of the
> wave? (*16*)

The man overboard is grotesquely stopped in that horizontal pendulum swing, held there as he is buffeted by wind and wave. However right his intentions, he is caught in mortal motion. In this position, he is himself part of the chaos; he figures, perhaps, the false, the misleading start, no less than do the repeated deflections of the poem from its end and the repeated interpretations of event that begin again and again.

The speaker's struggle to find the word goes on, tensed against the knowledge of the nun's triumphant finding. That tension is mitigated but never obliterated by the consciousness that, for all the poem's mimesis, for all its struggle, poetry is not for Hopkins the real event. The reader senses that interpretation, after all its struggle to become event, is not allowed to be event—the poem is not the place to enact religious salvation.

Stanza twenty-seven, reflective in mode, is an explanation that reveals the failure of analysis to reach the eye of the storm, the nun's emotional center:

> No, but it was not these.
> The jading and jar of the cart,
> Time's tasking, it is fathers that asking for ease
> Of the sodden-with-its-sorrowing heart,
> Not danger, electrical horror; then further it finds
> The appealing of the Passion is tenderer in prayer apart:
> Other, I gather, in measure her mind's
> Burden, in wind's burly and beat of endragonèd seas.

The negatives, hesitations, qualifications, and willed turnings away ("No, but it was not these"; "Other, I gather, in measure her mind's / Burden") prepare for a greater turning in the poem as the speaker rejects the readiest explanations and tries to grasp what happened.

Stanza twenty-eight then abandons reflection about the event, trying to plunge back into the experience, trying to understand in another way. The speaker now tries to find the word that is Christ as the nun found the word, in the present tense. This new reading, in other words, announces itself as no reading—or as a reading that is not the experience of reading but actually *is* the experience it is reading. The language apparently proceeds from the assumption that the speaker—here and now in the poem—can read the nun's event as the nun read the storm and so find the vision (word) that the nun may have found. The stanza claims to be repetition.[9] But in spite of all its apparent claims, the language of stanza twenty-eight does not allow interpretation to become event:

> But how shall I . . . make me room there:
> Reach me a . . . Fancy, come faster—
> Strike you the sight of it? look at it loom there,
> Thing that she . . . There then! the Master,
> *Ipse*, the only one, Christ, King, Head:
> He was to cure the extremity where he had cast her;
> Do, deal, lord it with living and dead;
> Let him ride, her pride, in his triumph, despatch and have done
> with his doom there.

The speaker at the start of this stanza consciously abandons his previous spelling of the nun's mind and tries himself to repeat her event on the page. But the pauses and half-articulated questions and syntactical leavings are all rather bald, even mechanical.[10] The I/you disjunction, so successful elsewhere, here seems too insistent and self-conscious. In the fact of its presence, the I/you disjunction gives evidence that the discrete moment is neither unified nor charged by the larger force of Christ. The "you" here glances rather awkwardly at the reader, seeming to ask if he too 'sees.' Finally, and probably most fatally, "Fancy, come faster" is patent and half-hearted artifice when placed beside the urgency of the nun's cry, " 'O Christ, Christ, come quickly' " (24). The speaker is nowhere in the poem, I think, more caught in his own artifice, and it is at least possible that he is nowhere more aware of being so caught. That is, it is likely, given the triviality of "Fancy, come faster," that Hopkins is consciously forbidding the poem to be event. (It is also worth remembering that the subordination of fancy, mere inventiveness, to imagination, creation, had been current at least since the Romantics and that this is the only occurrence of the word "fancy" in Hopkins' mature poetry.)

With "There then!" the speaker tells us that he has achieved his objective, the sight of Christ—a self-conscious revelation at best.

After the fine string of appositives naming Christ, he returns to his more familiar stance, considering Christ in relation to the other—in the imperative.

Repeatedly, we have seen Hopkins' ability to leave us, even in the midst of discovery, poised at the brink of further discovery. We have seen his way of pointing his speaker—physically, mentally, emotionally—in a specific direction. In the utmost clarity of found religious truth, the speaker is yet in anticipation, yet on the way to the further finding. In much of the poetry the sense of being so poised and so pointed tenses against the didactic ontology of the speaker. The speaker repeatedly finds himself at the moment of dawning, the moment before the greater clarity, a moment of clarity within itself but whose motion is always still on the way to more wondrous revision. Christ is not so much reached as he is reached for. Even the nun's cry, for all its aura of vision and miracle is yet uncertain in Hopkins' reading, strongly embodying suggestion and hope for the speaker but yet uncertain: "The majesty! what did she mean?" (25). In sharp contrast, if we are to take the speaker at his word in stanza twenty-eight, he has literally called his God into being: "There then! the Master, / *Ipse*, the only one, Christ, King, Head." It is as if the attempt to become the nightingale or the west wind had actually worked. There is no failure admitted here, nor any dwelling in loss. Instead, the speaker goes on quickly to ask that his risen lord, *Ipse*, complete his triumphant scene in the poem. Even at that, the speaker phrases part of his petition in the third person and, far from being caught in a present vision, focuses on Christ's relation to the nun.

Indeed, it is now, in stanzas twenty-nine and thirty, that the nun is most strongly connected with *her* finding of the "right" word, a finding kept sharply distinct from the speaker's self: "Ah! *there* was a heart right! / *There* was single eye!" (italics added). This is a recognizable Hopkins, seeing Christ in the other, excitedly reading his text. Stanza twenty-eight, perhaps, is meant to guess at what might have happened; it is not meant to repeat the happening.

If the speaker has failed to enact the nun's event, he has communicated well the difficulty of knowing that event—"(And here the faithful waver, the faithless fable and miss)"—as well as the difficulty of seeking out language. The nun's language forms a vestige or trace of the heart's event because it is all that remains of what may have been miracle, revelation. (In fact, part of her specialness is that her breaking gives off language, intelligible sign.) The word that breaks from her heart at stress becomes the object of the speaker's consideration through time; the language flung out during her selving becomes the object of the speaker's study. A contrast of language, then, occurs between the two uses of the word—between the nun's word, spoken, spontaneous, and the speaker's word, studied, prolonged; between the nun who breaks open from within, into language, and the speaker who starts with her word and struggles to break through language to the experience of the heart.

As interesting as it is, stanza twenty-eight is not the heart of the speaker's experience in the poem. As in "Felix Randal" and "Spring and Fall," the speaker centers his own experience in the center of the poem. At the spatial center of the *Deutschland*, in stanza number eighteen of thirty-five, occurs the most extended poetic signal of the ongoing struggle with language. Stanza eighteen sharply breaks into the poem's plot; it daringly interrupts the story of the shipwreck in the pitch of the tumult during the first approach to the nun's word.

The stanza is reflexive, spoken by the speaker to himself:

> Ah, touched in your bower of bone,
> Are you! turned for an exquisite smart,
> Have you! make words break from me here all alone,
> Do you!—mother of being in me, heart.
> O unteachably after evil, but uttering truth,
> Why, tears! is it? tears; such a melting, a madrigal start!
> Never-eldering revel and river of youth,
> What can it be, this glee? the good you have there of your own?

At the start of the stanza, the speaker is self-involved and mockingly amused at his own emotion in response to the story he tells ("with the heart-break hearing a heart-broke rabble" [17]). 'Now,' he seems to say, 'finally you are moved to the good.' But the exclamations grow insistent, seemingly flung by the speaker at self;

the "you" in its jarring position returns again and again. The reader experiences "Are you!" as a twisting of syntax that stresses the speaker's surprise and hints at the self-mockery at work, but its recurrence in "Have you!" is more obstinate in its emphasis on tone, turning that mockery into something harder, a harsher re-flexive irony. For one thing, "Have you!" is unnecessary to the referential sense of the language; joined by alliteration, syntactical pattern, and rhythms almost exactly the same, "touched in your bower of bone" and "turned for an exquisite smart" both seem to feed off "Are you!" The caesura after the second line is more decisive, noticeably longer, than that after the first, and "Have you!"—because of the longer pause—strikes with increased force even as it is more dislocated and awkward in syntax. And then the speaker does it yet again, saying, "make words break from me here all alone, / Do you!" This final recurrence puts even more stress on the exclamation: The "you!" is even more strongly em-phasized than before, the self more hopelessly divided. In these three and one-half lines, the tension thus rises; there is a turning of the screw, an increasing tightness of the self. What starts out as self-pointing half in disbelief and almost ironic in tone becomes, through insistent recurrence, an edged self-accusation and then an almost helpless cry at the speaker's own helplessness.

But all of the pressure self-inflicted, the tautness and the antag-onism, and even the sense of helplessness (his increased passivity, his sense of being acted upon)—all of this wholly dissolves at the center, dissolves to an intimacy, a tenderness extended to and emerging from the self, a tenderness which names the addressee, the actor—his own being, *his* center:

—mother of being in me, heart.

After that tight, insistent "you!" these words go slack, seeming to move into the center they name, which is the origin of all pressure and of all words breaking forth. "Heart" emerges as pure breath, and for a moment the narrative is no longer 'about' anything. Without gap between past event and present saying, there is no otherness, and all otherness gone, the immediate saying *is* the event. At one with the emerging self, the language touches its own

154

hidden center. Before and behind *The Wreck of the Deutschland* is "mother of being in me, heart."

Possibly, this is the center of the poem because, in the speaker's mind, it is the center of the world, it is providence in the world. The nature of providence in the world conceals essential being, conceals the goodness of things within a hidden center that emerges from its hiding only at rare times in response to fortuitous event. Thus, God himself in the poem is a "sovereignty that heeds but hides" (32), and Christ is "Our passion-plungèd giant risen" (33), sprung up from the depths. The nun's word is "heart-throe, birth of a brain" (30); the speaker himself has, in his moment of assent, whirled out dovewings from a heart swooning, trod by God (2–3); and "only the heart, being hard at bay, / Is out with it!" (7–8). The sloe breaking open serves as figure for all goodness in being:

> How a lush-kept plush-capped sloe
> Will, mouthed to flesh-burst,
> Gush!—flush the man, the being with it, sour or sweet,
> Brim, in a flash, full! (8)

The hidden center emerges under pressure, like the "juice and joy" of "Spring," providence known.

For even in a poem that turns on the word, a poem whose impetus is a word, language is precious primarily for what it signals, its reference. The heart, the hidden heart, is primary, and its language is not always—nor even mostly—verbal: "What by your measure is the heaven of desire, / The treasure never eyesight got, nor was ever guessed what for the hearing?" (26). God is "Beyond saying sweet, past telling of tongue" (9). Both the speaker's past assent and the nun's assent sprang from the heart. In fact, the language of the speaker's past assent, the expression of self at the time of his turning, was not verbal language at all: "I did say yes / O at lightning and lashed rod; / Thou heardst me *truer than tongue* confess / Thy terror, O Christ, O God" (2) (italics added). The description locates a more genuine language, unfalsifiable, in the fact that the earlier event was inarticulate. As with Margaret's weeping, the absence of words validates the event's primal importance.

Now, in the saying of the poem, the speaker confronts that first experience, only now meeting it with verbal language, confirming it with the very words that were unnecessary during the experience: "My heart, but you were dovewinged, *I can tell,* / Carrier-witted, *I am bold to boast*" (3) (italics added). But the essential self of that essential turning toward God was without words. The "swoon of a heart" (2) said yes then, and Hopkins now articulates the remembered crisis as physical motions propelled by the heart. The heart, "Carrier-witted," "dovewinged," flashed and towered, flung itself to the Host's heart, enacted a redemptive reciprocity that alone relieved the physical discomfort, the sense of frantic dislocation.

The nun, in contrast, merges the word with her event or even, perhaps, fulfills the event in the word. She "Has one fetch in her: she rears herself to divine / Ears, and the call of the tall nun / To the men in the tops and the tackle rode over the storm's brawling" (19). The call is still appended to the gestural action, but that expression of selving may well have towered her to the further grace, the final and miraculous incarnation. For the nun it is not tears which emerge, and her word goes far beyond the unformulated "Áh!" of the "Spring and Fall" speaker. "'O Christ, Christ, come quickly'" (24) selves finally and awfully into words, and the words themselves prove a further hidden center for the poet.

To the speaker, the word, her word, "'O Christ, Christ, come quickly,'" is the ultimate clarity which is incomprehensible. The word sprung from the nun's extreme selving is to the speaker a vestige, a trace of the heart's unknowable event. "The majesty! what did she mean?" (25) breathes the speaker. And while many stanzas try to answer that difficult question, the word continues to exist as mysterious sign, finally indecipherable. The nun's language, seemingly determinable, relapses in those stanzas of exploration into the process of the speaker's mind. Indeed, as this drama of the speaker's process suggests, "what did she mean?" must finally refer not only to 'what did her words mean?' but to 'what did *she* mean?' As the following stanzas develop, the speaker questions the meaning of the nun's being, her meaning to self, speaker, God, and England. *Her* word is not detachable from her heart; it is "arch and original Breath" (25).

It is thus that Hopkins' "passion for explanation" triumphs, willing the storm, now a fortuitous event instead of a tragic one, into blessing, providential event: "For I greet him the days I meet him, and bless when I understand" (5). Possibly, the fortuitous event in Hopkins is always willed into the providential event, greeting made blessing. The will to discovery forms an undercurrent of pressure in all the poems, even in the sonnets of desolation. Often, that will forms the line of time, as if the poem cannot fulfill itself or end until the attention held reveals explanation, understanding, blessing—"shéer plód makes plough down sillion / Shine" ("The Windhover").

In recounting his past turning, the speaker reveals that the hidden center emerged, broke out in response to God's pressure, a destructive and terrifying pressure turned life giving and blessed. This was the fortuitous discovery, both analogue and prologue to the nun's discovery. In other places, though, discovery seems more willed, driven by human action. In stanza five, the speaker's gesture of kissing his hand to the stars elicits Christ's emergence in thunder:

> I kiss my hand
>   To the stars, lovely-asunder
>   Starlight, wafting him out of it; and
>   Glow, glory in thunder;
>   Kiss my hand to the dappled-with-damson west:
>   Since, tho' he is under the world's splendour and wonder,
>   His mystery must be instressed, stressed;
> For I greet him the days I meet him, and bless when I understand.

The speaker does not realize the sought-after encounter every time he actively searches one out—the failure to discover finally and exactly what the nun 'meant' is the most extended example of the unrealized encounter in the poem. Still, the effort is not lost, for the nun's word is transformed through poetic process into another kind of discovery, although perhaps not the one the speaker was looking for. His original aim, to uncover the meaning of the nun's event to the nun, is deflected, and he turns, instead, to the hope that that unexplained event may foreshadow the larger conversion of England.

In a sense, then, the will to discovery is the shaping force guiding the poem. The intervention of Part the First to precede Part the Second disorders narrative chronology and makes the present moment of saying into an ordering rather than a mere recounting. Thus, the poem in its structure tells us that the sign's importance inheres in its pervasiveness in history and time: "Over again I feel thy finger and find thee" (1). That the fortuitous encounter happens "over again"—over and over again—affirms the providential presence. It affirms lasting over passing, the ongoing recurrence over the awful absence. The present saying of past event is a finding again, a recurrence of the event happening now within the poem. The poem is its own willed discovery.

The voice insists on necessity. Hopkins would have us believe that the providential presence is there because it is also there, and there, and because it recurs, in past, present, and future. Because the personal self can merge into the historical self, because one's own assent can date "from day / Of his going in Galilee" (7), because the speaker can find himself anew while reading the experience of the nun—because of all these things and more, Hopkins affirms that the directional force of Christ revises mortal chronology. The poem resists the isolation of event even as it resists the exquisite utterance, the unrecurring uniqueness. (That it does so resist makes the possibility of miracle within the nun's vision all the more wonderful.) "I did say yes" (2) wills a fresh assent even as it rebounds and resounds its assent to past assent. Hopkins resists ultimate isolation because even within the plenitude of the recurring world, even within the plenitude of the fortuitous event always urging us to read providence in the world, the final overflowing that would engulf all single selves never occurs. This is the absence in the midst of Hopkins' riches: In the onrush of words, in the onrush of event in the storm itself, there is still a tautness, a leaving sensed from a distance as an emancipation that cannot be willed.

For again, the deepest experience is by nature unprolongable and must be sought out again and again. Hopkins' poetry feels the loss and strives toward the re-finding—again and again. The speaker's is a "motionable mind" (32), and it informs a poetry that is "mined [mind] with a motion, a drift" (4).

The language insists on this motion of mind as much as it does on any stated subject:

> —mother of being in me, heart.
> O unteachably after evil, but uttering truth,
> Why, tears! is it? tears; such a melting, a madrigal start!
> Never-eldering revel and river of youth,
> What can it be, this glee? the good you have there of your
> own?

At the center of stanza eighteen, "heart" is held, "heart" hangs there in its close oneness of self, only to fall as it slides into the explanatory cry "O unteachably after evil, but uttering truth." These words try to reach out, to hold on to "heart," accepting and yet pitying and regretting the ambiguity of self in their recognition, in their naming, in their O-ing. But even that attempt is lost when the surprise that is now no surprise pulls the speaker up short: "Why, tears! is it? tears."

The voice is falling back further and further from the experience in its commenting *on* the experience, and growing more crowded and faster in its fall. It stops to exclaim on that new start, tumbles to the intellected and elaborate naming of the tear (itself a new start although it again tries to hold on), and finally subsides into the language of simple prose, a prose that finds itself far away from its origin in "heart."

Moved far from the 'pure' experience of "heart," the speaker in the last line questions more consciously the meaning of the nun's cry; the words are falling away from event and toward spelled meaning, although not into it. The speaker's questioning of self, harsh and derisive in the stanza's first half, has become a questioning of self and word and object. Here, within the approach to the nun's word, he has a premonition of present involvement, an important relation among self, nun, and the word engendered by the process of poetry.

The subtle relation of self to word and object hints at the process which generates the poem's drama and so implies the reader's experience too. The speaker's process of mind and language is a soft sift, a fluctuating and indeterminable motion; that motion poses significant questions even as it defies clear answers. Stanza eighteen explicitly challenges the relation of self to word and object and, in so doing, brings forth questions underlying the whole *Deutschland* and, indeed, the entire poetic of Hopkins' poetry. Is the self most real when it is emerging, breaking from, that hidden center, or is it most real in its discovery of order (Christ) in the world? Is the poem most real at that moment of experience, loss, or at the moment of recognition, formulation, understanding of loss? And how does Hopkins embody the process which transmutes the sign, the object, and the self into one another?

In Romantic poetry, it is the moment of experience—realization, emergence, transmittal—that has meaning and must pass into loss. The event of the poem saves (preserves) the poet's saying of presence and loss. This is in contrast to the linear Christian millennium and its dynamic driving toward an ultimate (inevitable) end—Hopkins must find Christ in the world, not in his own words. He must ostensibly negate poetry as salvation, must subordinate the poetic transubstantiation: His propounded salvational line is external and independent of poetic act, linear and indestructible. Supposedly, it is the external meaning, sign, symbol, event that saves the temporal world. Doctrinally, man is loss, lost, losing, and the exterior event, the Holy Ghost brooding over a bent world, saves that loss.

But that is dogma. In fact, in the poem, despite the ultimate determinable meanings of salvation read in the world, despite the poet's reading of nun, England, and the self emerged and projected as sign, it is the poet's voice that takes the event, sign, symbol, forges its determinable meaning, and brings it back into the soft sift of the voice's struggle. There, it is lost again, lost in the intertwining of dialectic rumination, consideration, and meditation—and all those in their mental and emotional, conscious and unconscious weavings. This process, the process of the self's struggle, may yield new symbol, larger reading. And this new symbol is itself subject to the process again, subject to the loss and transformed emergence, stirring out of its hiding to appear as yet larger symbol, Christ at the nearer doorstep.

In this sense, the real dramatic event of the *Deutschland* is not the nun's cry but the speaker's motions into and out of that event. The first event of the self, the speaker's retelling of his own past assent, moves from the individual and personal to become the larger symbol of Christ's mastery in the world through time. The assent is itself but more than itself. Then, brought back into process, it is lost, transformed into and displaced by the nun's event, which is itself and becoming more than itself. Then her event is brought back into the questioning uncertainty of the speaker's voice only to emerge again, transmuted into the still larger event, explicitly Christ saving England, but implicitly Christ saving the world, validating linear time and externality.

Yet validating externality, validating the symbolic structure of the poem, is somewhat at odds with the process through which the poem is created. Admittedly or not, it is the poetry that knows (finds, loses, transforms, re-signs) the event. If it is not the autonomous imagination, then it is at least, although not to be boasted of, poetic process that makes the sign real and knowable; it is the poetic process from which the event emerges as sign.

The symbol undergoes process, determination, loss, and emergence. More essentially, the voice struggles with those palpable moments when meaning is emerging or disintegrating. The poem's event is not only its propaganda, what it says it is about, its hard determination of symbolic presence. The poem's dramatic event is also its happening, its process—not hard like the shard of determination, but a struggle of the voice of the motionable self as it falls through time in and out, into and out of objective meaning. The real dramatic event of the poem is the voice's struggle to save the loss, whether moving toward hard meaning, symbol, or away from it. When determinable meaning is confounded in interpretation, while the symbol is mined, the soft sift, the process, the tacit knowing that is un-knowing, becomes the hard knowing.

Stanza two, which purportedly recalls a past event, illustrates well the conflict between the poem's ostensible subject and the speaker's process:

> I did say yes
> O at lightning and lashed rod;

> Thou heardst me truer than tongue confess
> Thy terror, O Christ, O God;
> Thou knowest the walls, altar and hour and night:
> The swoon of a heart that the sweep and the hurl of thee
>   trod
> Hard down with a horror of height:
> And the midriff astrain with leaning of, laced with fire of
>   stress.

Initially, the stanza is a revisitation, a meeting of the past primary experience with the word: a secondary event. "I did say yes," the speaker says, and his diction and syntax, his stressed simplicity and directness, his prosaic language, are all apart from his original experience even as they reaffirm it. His words are revisionary, not visionary, attempting to retrace through assertion what remains of the event now largely concealed; but implicitly, they hope to reinvoke the lost experience and validate its significance or primacy.

The extreme control and direction asserted over the past event do not last. The language soon finds itself struggling with its own significance. In the struggle to authenticate itself, articulate language breaks and in its breaking reforms grammar and syntax—almost as if to indicate that the present poetic act of speech is under an intense and breaking pressure similar to that which yielded the original experience. "O at lightning and lashed rod" gives evidence that the language is already under a reforming pressure, subject to and shaped by an immediate impulse that alters the previous impulse of the speaker. The "O" falls out of the discipline of "I did say yes"; "lashed" is an adjective, an elaboration of language compared to the spare syntax of the stanza's first line, an elaboration apparently emerging from the pressure of sound, the temptation to alliterate with "lightning"; the "at" (instead of 'to') gives evidence that conflict is present now. Whatever the initial willed intent to speak, the willed intent is interrupted and altered by an impulse (seemingly unpremeditated, unintentional) that swerves in another direction. Language, at first meant to define a past presence, itself takes precedence, filling the vacancies created by the presence of loss. The saying intended as secondary becomes primary process.

The repetition and naming in line four, "O Christ, O God,"

decelerates the hectic onrush of language and feeling that threatens
to engulf all, redirecting the stanza back toward its planned design.
"Thou knowest" continues the new externality, the definiteness
and direction of "O Christ, O God." But the reforming pressure
reasserts itself, and language as primary process again gains the
ascendency over the past event: Once again, the energy of the
poem makes itself known in successive waves that deflect and re-
vise prior intention or direction:

> Thou knowest the walls, altar and hour and night:
> The swoon of a heart that the sweep and the hurl of thee
>   trod
>   Hard down with a horror of height:
> And the midriff astrain with leaning of, laced with fire of
>   stress.
>
> The frown of his face
> Before me, the hurtle of hell
> Behind, where, where was a, where was a place?
> I whirled out wings that spell
> And fled with a fling of the heart to the heart of the Host.
>
> *(2–3)*

The violent acceleration and deceleration of spoken language in
stanzas two and three suggest impending annihilation. Possibly, it
is because of this threatened destruction that the act of speech
becomes the actual constituting of self. What is becoming present
is the speaker's self at the very edge of existence: "The hurtle of
hell / Behind, where, where was a, where was a place?" At mo-
ments such as this, language is becoming more than sign because
it is overrun by the act of speaking, an act in which the energy
forming the word is more present than the word it forms. Such
moments are marked by a real exhilaration of language and self
as they begin to defy the world. The exhilaration of the language
of despair in "Spelt from Sibyl's Leaves" and in the sonnets of
desolation is like this; and throughout the poetry, the speaker's
interjections, his 'Ahs' and 'Os,' and his moments when chaos
seems to have come again, are times when the qualities of other-
ness and sign are obscured and language is no longer put forth as

a mediation between the self and the world. But such moments do not create 'unmediated visions' because visions demand concreteness, representation, referential and formed qualities within the mind. In the threat of formlessness when the activity of speaking is most disposed toward obliterating form and coherent meaning, the possibilities of a coalescence of self and word arise, a coalescence that increasingly precludes the world, ostensible reference, or any other denoted pre-existing thing or thought.

The energies of poetic speech seen in stanzas two and three, the motions of direction and deflection, are re-enacted throughout the poem. They are recurrences not of language but of the activity of speaking. Moreover, the shape of the stanza accommodates poetic speaking, with the shorter lines of the stanza's start gradually yielding to the long line of the stanza's close. Hopkins was never again to allow himself a stanzaic form with nearly so much invitation for language to overtake direction and meaning, a form in which the overtaking so readily becomes a dramatic process. The reader comes to sense and recognize a recurring pattern of activity as the language asserting control over word and world at the stanza's start gives way to an act of speaking that insists on itself and its own making of self at the stanza's close. The stanza's form so welcomes the liberation of language—until the next stanza, with its opening short line, provides a constraint that returns the voice to its narrative, linear function:

> Into the snows she sweeps,
> Hurling the haven behind,
> The Deutschland, on Sunday; and so the sky keeps,
> For the infinite air is unkind,
> And the sea flint-flake, black-backed in the regular blow,
> Sitting Eastnortheast, in cursed quarter, the wind;
> Wiry and white-fiery and whirlwind-swivellèd snow
> Spins to the widow-making unchilding unfathering deeps.
>
> She drove in the dark to leeward,
> She struck—not a reef or a rock
> But the combs of a smother of sand: night drew her
> Dead to the Kentish Knock;

And she beat the bank down with her bows and the ride
  of her keel;
The breakers rolled on her beam with ruinous shock;
And canvas and compass, the whorl and the wheel
Idle for ever to waft her or wind her with, these she endured.

(13, 14)

The *Deutschland* stanza fairly demands that the lyricism overcome the design. Although the stanza's beginning may anchor the onrush temporarily, the paragraph's length is long, and the reader comes to expect not only the deluge of imagery at the end but the activity of language that seems to be losing control, hastening sometimes in spite of its intentions directly into that deluge. Even "Spelt from Sibyl's Leaves" with its 8-foot lines does not dramatize the activity of language in this way because its lines are equal in length, because its shape does not plan for the recurrent waves, lyricism over and over engulfing design.

The reader of the *Deutschland* knows the activity of language, poetic speaking, familiarly although not consciously, in his continual engagement with the poem. The reader's identity, however, is discrete from the speaker's intimate involvement with language. But for both speaker and reader, the activity of language, poetic speaking, is 'known' as it emerges from concealment—or more precisely, as it is emerging from concealment. For the speaker, poetic speaking is emerging from the concealment of his own interior and unforethought of existence; and for the reader, who is reading the word as the speaker reads the world, poetic speaking is emerging from the concealment of language as sign. The two emergings are necessarily different.

Ostensibly about the right reading of signs, the decoding of the world, *The Wreck of the Deutschland* is at least as much concerned with the human making of signs, with the unmaking, and with the remaking. The significances, the meanings of the poem, ride between those determinable and determined signs and the less ostensible and less determinable but ever-present making of sign and meaning: between the apparent real and the hidden emerging, shaping itself real.

Abbreviations

Poems
: *The Poems of Gerard Manley Hopkins*. Eds. W. H. Gardner and Norman H. MacKenzie. 4th ed. 1967. Reprint. London: Oxford University Press, 1970.

Journals
: *The Journals and Papers of Gerard Manley Hopkins*. Eds. Humphry House and Graham Storey. London: Oxford University Press, 1959.

Sermons
: *The Sermons and Devotional Writings of Gerard Manley Hopkins*. Ed. Christopher Devlin, S.J. London: Oxford University Press, 1959.

Letters 1
: *The Letters of Gerard Manley Hopkins to Robert Bridges*. Ed. Claude Colleer Abbott. 1935. Rev. imp. London: Oxford University Press, 1955.

Letters 2
: *The Correspondence of Gerard Manley Hopkins and Richard Watson Dixon*. Ed. Claude Colleer Abbott. 1935. Rev. imp. London: Oxford University Press, 1955.

Letters 3
: *Further Letters of Gerard Manley Hopkins Including His Correspondence with Coventry Patmore*. Ed. Claude Colleer Abbott. 2d ed. London: Oxford University Press, 1956.

HQ
: *The Hopkins Quarterly*

Notes

I. Gestures of Assent

1. For discussion of Wordsworth's reflexive consciousness, see Albert O. Wlecke, *Wordsworth and the Sublime*, esp. 21–46 on "Tintern Abbey." Hopkins' references and allusions to Wordsworth are many. An Oxford essay, "Poetic Diction," is based on Wordsworth; the poem "Brothers" has connections to Wordsworth's poem of the same name (see *Letters* 1: 106); a light verse, " 'The Child is Father to the Man,' " mocks Wordsworth's line. In the letters, Hopkins says that when Wordsworth wrote the "Immortality Ode," "human nature got another of those shocks, and the tremble from it is spreading" (*Letters* 2: 148). But he objects to the poetry's lack of disciplined form and says that Wordsworth's sonnets "suffer from 'hernia', and combine the tiro's blunder with the master's perfection" (*Letters* 2: 142). For some of the other comments on Wordsworth, see *Letters* 1: 38, 211; *Letters* 2: 141; *Letters* 3: 219–20, 229, 355.

2. M. H. Abrams, *Natural Supernaturalism*, 94. See also 46–70 on the development of a 'natural' religion and 119–22 on the poet as prophet. For the idea of poetic power in Wordsworth's "Essay, Supplementary to the Preface," see W. J. B. Owen, *Wordsworth as Critic*, 195–228.

3. See Robert Langbaum, *The Poetry of Experience*, 20–28.

4. *Letters* 2: 98.

5. *Letters* 1: 61.

6. See, for examples, *Letters* 1: 65–66 (to Bridges); *Letters* 2:

169

88, 93–94, and passim, 92–99. At first, Hopkins seems to enjoy the idea of publishing in religious journals, but the decision, once made, holds fast. Daniel A. Harris suggests that Hopkins' decision not to publish helped make the writing of poetry more acceptable to him. *Inspirations Unbidden,* 130–31.

7. See, for example, Michael Sprinker's *"A Counterpoint of Dissonance,"* which, although not concerned with the Romantics, locates the essential Hopkins in expressionistic ideas. For Sprinker, poetic writing in Hopkins is selving, creation of self; "As kingfishers catch fire" is a central text; and the poet's creative will argues throughout the canon with the need for submission. Thus, the career records Hopkins' increasing oppression with the 'prison house' of language, with his growing realization that the written text cannot *be* speech, and with the gradual disintegration of poetic will. The Miltonic plainness of some late poems shows the poet's abandonment of self to the anxiety of influence: "By capitulating to Milton's example, Hopkins ceases to be himself" and "Hopkins' poetry has become a feeble imitation of Milton" (144). The baroque writing of other late poems swerves in the opposite direction, with poetic individualism overwhelming the subject; and "in 'To R. B.,' Hopkins condemns himself to death as a poet" (129).

8. Carl Woodring has the fullest discussion of the extreme political consciousness of the Romantics in his *Politics in English Romantic Poetry.*

9. *Letters* 2: 93.

10. *Letters* 1: 66; *Letters* 2: 89.

11. *Letters* 2: 146.

12. *Letters* 1: 152.

13. *Letters* 1: 84.

14. *Journals,* 126; *Sermons,* 129.

15. Helen Gardner, *Religion and Literature,* 135; 134.

16. Hopkins speaks of Herbert only briefly, but about Vaughan he writes: "He has more glow and freedom than Herbert but less fragrant sweetness. . . . Still, I do not think him Herbert's equal" (*Letters* 2: 24).

Louis L. Martz yokes the poetry of Herbert and Hopkins under the rubric of his title, *The Poetry of Meditation.* His definition is structural (the recurring pattern of memory—understanding—will) and not necessarily religious; Helen Gardner's essay is rigorously limited to the poetry of defined religious outlook. See Martz, 322–25, and Helen Gardner, *Religion and Literature*, 186–89, on the two poets. For other mention of Hopkins and Herbert, see Joan Bennett, *Five Metaphysical Poets*, 65–67; Helen Vendler, *The Poetry of George Herbert*, 86–87; and W. H. Gardner, *Gerard Manley Hopkins: A Study*, 2: 73–74.

17. Another interesting parallel is that both wrote in relative obscurity, choosing not to seek publication during life. One has the sense that Herbert, much more than Hopkins, consciously intended his work to be published. He shaped the volume carefully and left it to a friend, asking that he decide whether it was worthy of publication. Hopkins may have had a similar plan in mind as he looked over the copies of his poems that Bridges had made. In 1879 he wrote to Bridges: "All therefore that I think of doing is to keep my verses together in one place—at present I have not even correct copies—, that, if anyone shd. like, they might be published after my death" (*Letters* 1: 66). Furthermore, Hopkins left his papers to the Society of Jesus, but the poetry went to Bridges.

18. For some verbal parallels, see W. H. Gardner, *Hopkins: A Study*, 1: 171–72.

19. Helen Gardner, *Religion and Literature*, 172; 187.

20. Herbert's poetry is "consciously and steadily directed toward resolution and integration" (L. C. Knights, "George Herbert," 138). See also Martz, *Poetry of Meditation*, 135; Bennett, *Five Metaphysical Poets*, 66. On the relation between the structural order of the Herbert poem and a higher order, see Joseph H. Summers, *George Herbert: His Religion and Art*, 73–95, but esp. 92–94; on allegory in Herbert, see 171–81.

21. Rosemond Tuve details the rich density of allusion and meaning in *A Reading of George Herbert*; see esp. 1–99, an essay on "The Sacrifice."

22. See Joan Webber, *The Eloquent "I,"* 5–11, for discussion of this in seventeenth-century Anglican prose.

23. On Hopkins' detailed vision, see Carol T. Christ, *The Finer Optic*, 95–104 and 127–49. She sees that "the Romantic poets transform natural objects into symbols, but Hopkins's ag-

gressive particularity implies a refusal to allow this transformation" (146–47). For Patricia M. Ball, Hopkins reconciles a Coleridgean Romanticism of reaction to the world with Ruskin's demand for accuracy of observation (*The Science of Aspects*, 103–50, esp. 141–47).

24. Langbaum, *Poetry of Experience*, 25.

25. *Sermons*, 123.

26. See Geoffrey Grigson, *Gerard Manley Hopkins*, 17, and Ball, *Science of Aspects*, 106, for strong statements of the Hopkins' speaker as a separated observer of the world.

27. John Henry Cardinal Newman, *An Essay in Aid of a Grammar of Assent*, 90. Todd K. Bender relates Newman's real assent to the method of *The Spiritual Exercises* (*Gerard Manley Hopkins: The Classical Background*, 148–49); Christ speaks of the aridity of notional assent and necessity for particular experience (*Finer Optic*, 144–45). Norman H. MacKenzie names the *Grammar* as an important influence on an 1885 lecture ("The Imperative Voice—An Unpublished Lecture by Hopkins," 107–8). Finally, Michael D. Moore works more generally with Newman and Hopkins, finding echoes and parallels between a variety of Newman's writings and Hopkins' poetry.

28. Newman, *Grammar*, 32; 36; 47.

29. See *Letters* 3: 412.

30. *Journals*, 127.

31. In this sense all active verbs subordinate their subjects to some degree, but Hopkins' use of simple verbs directly following simple subjects in a poetry that elsewhere abounds with modifiers and unusual syntax seems to stress the subordination. Josephine Miles noted early on that "Hopkins is short on straight active verb forms, despite the general impression of many readers" ("The Sweet and Lovely Language," 64). Surely one reason for that "general impression" is that the straight, active verb forms, when they do occur, are made to carry such weight.

32. For discussion of "indistinctness and the subconscious" in Coleridge's aesthetics, see J. A. Appleyard, S.J., *Coleridge's Philosophy of Literature*, 86–93.

33. See Geoffrey H. Hartman, *The Unmediated Vision*, 49–60, for more on the physicality of Hopkins' poetry.

34. Robert J. Dilligan and Todd K. Bender cite, in their *Concordance to the English Poetry of Gerard Manley Hopkins,* sixty-eight uses of "heart," the most frequently used noun in the poetry; when plurals, possessives, compounds, and other forms are added, the number rises to more than a hundred. "Heart" pervades the poetry.

35. On the linearity of Christian time, see Mircea Eliade, *The Myth of the Eternal Return,* 143. Octavio Paz, in *Children of the Mire,* writes of the Romantic idea of time shaping a modern world of endless flux (31–57).

36. *Sermons,* 239.

37. Victor Zuckerkandl has a relevant discussion of directional force in music in his *Sound and Symbol;* see esp. the whole section on tonal motion, 1: 74–148.

38. Hartman, *Unmediated Vision,* 53.

39. Newman, *Grammar,* 163: "Certitude . . . is the perception of a truth with the perception that it is a truth, or the consciousness of knowing, as expressed in the phrase, 'I know that I know.'"

40. *Sermons,* 174.

41. Wendell Stacy Johnson comments on "ah my dear": "It can refer to the bird, or to Christ 'my chevalier,' or just possibly to the poet himself (although Hopkins does not seem elsewhere to use this Henry Jamesian form) or possibly to the reader, the imagined audience." Johnson's conclusion suggests that all possibilities are included in the phrase, but he places some emphasis on the reader; in any case, he is right I think to single out the "phrase perhaps more ambiguous than some more often debated" (*Gerard Manley Hopkins: The Poet as Victorian,* 95). Both Johnson (95) and W. H. Gardner (Notes to *Poems,* 268) note Herbert's use of the phrase in "Love (II)."

42. Joseph Eble, "Levels of Awareness," 132.

43. *Letters* 1: 56.

44. *Journals,* 228.

45. But see also Jerome Bump's discussion, based in "Rosa Mystica," which finds that the imagery's "multiple vertical correspondences" approximate medieval typology. Bump also writes that Hopkins often reverses the normal metaphor with its "paral-

lelism in which the unknown is described in terms of the known to a sacramental symbol of convergence . . . in which the unknown meets and mixes with the known" ("Hopkins' Imagery and Medievalist Poetics," 118; idem, *Gerard Manley Hopkins,* 90).

46. Harris, in his book on the terrible sonnets, writes that "the poems occur in a universe whose theological structure, quite apart from the spiritual vicissitudes endured by Hopkins's speaker, is no longer secure" (*Inspirations Unbidden,* 113).

47. Wayne C. Booth ends his *Modern Dogma and the Rhetoric of Assent* in an affirmation of the processes of dialectic. Modernism here derives from the assumption of the absence of shared belief. But, as Booth holds, even the idea of the meaningless in twentieth-century literature includes the affirmation of trying to express meaninglessness.

Thus, within Hopkins' sonnets of desolation at their most terrible is the speaker's God-affirming despair of grace and the poet's activity of trying to say the horror.

48. Harris writes that "paradoxically . . . when Hopkins was too distraught to care at all for a fictive audience—in the 'terrible sonnets'—his poems became most directly accessible to the actual audience he never dared court" (*Inspirations Unbidden,* 138).

II. Lyricism and Design

1. In *Inscape: The Christology and Poetry of Gerard Manley Hopkins,* James Finn Cotter sees in the idea of fullness a mythopoetic scheme based on the Omega.

2. But characteristically, Hopkins may have had an actual weed in mind; see Paul L. Mariani's *Commentary on the Complete Poems of Gerard Manley Hopkins,* 100.

3. The poem here incorporates the reading marks of the A version recorded in Notes to *Poems,* 293.

4. *Letters* 1: 263. Mariani thinks the poem inspired by a painting: "Hopkins 'Harry Ploughman' and Frederick Walker's 'The Plough,' " 42–44.

5. Work, directed action, is to be valued: "It is not only prayer that gives God glory but work. . . . To lift up the hands in prayer gives God glory, but a man with a dungfork in his hand, a

woman with a sloppail, give him glory too" (*Sermons*, 240–41).
See, too, Robert Lowell, "Hopkins' Sanctity," 90–91, and Alison
G. Sulloway, *Gerard Manley Hopkins and the Victorian Temper*,
84. Work is self-sacrifice, and James Finn Cotter sees the plough-
man as an image of the crucified Christ in his "'Hornlight Wound
to the West,'" 309–10.

    6. *Letters* 2: 153; 1: 262.

    7. Elisabeth W. Schneider, *The Dragon in the Gate*, 11.

    8. For the strength of "simple *yes* and *is*," see *Journals*, 127.
Several critics have worked with the form of Ignatian medita-
tion in Hopkins' poems. The idea is thematic to David A. Downes'
Gerard Manley Hopkins: A Study of His Ignatian Spirit and Daniel
A. Harris' *Inspirations Unbidden*. (But Harris notes that the ap-
pearance of Ignatian structure in the poems precedes Hopkins'
entry into the Society of Jesus [88].) Cotter returns, throughout his
Inscape, to the intellectual and emotional influence of the *Spiritual
Exercises*, and Todd K. Bender compares Hopkins and Crashaw
in their use of Ignatian colloquy (*Gerard Manley Hopkins: The
Classical Background*, 137–68).

    9. For the poem's images, see Peter Milward, S.J. and Ray-
mond Schoder, S.J., *Landscape and Inscape*, and Norman H.
MacKenzie, *A Reader's Guide to Gerard Manley Hopkins*, 145–
48. It is interesting that Hopkins seems to have written an early
version of the last stanza quite apart from any specific scene; see
Letters 1: 73–74.

    10. Geoffrey H. Hartman, *The Unmediated Vision*, 49. Ex-
amining a *Journals* passage, Carol T. Christ contrasts Hopkins to
the Romantics when she observes that "Hopkins does not make his
wild flowers into symbols from which to ascend directly to heaven,
but apprehends their most minute particularity and suddenly leaps
to heaven" (*The Finer Optic*, 147).

    11. My discussion here and in the last section of this chapter
owes much to Murray Krieger's essay "*Ekphrasis* and the Still
Movement of Poetry: or *Laokoon* Revisited." *Ekphrasis* is here
the basic tension of every poem, the problem "of Keats with his
Grecian Urn: how to make it hold still when the poem must
move" (343).

    12. *Letters* 1: 275.

13. *Letters* 1: 202; 293.

14. First quotation, *Letters* 1: 272–73 (a page of explanation is omitted where the ellipsis points appear; the poem under discussion is "Tom's Garland"); second quotation, ibid., 177. For some of the other comments on the poems' intelligibility (or lack of it), see *Letters* 1: 78, 171, 174, 265.

15. *Letters* 1: 265.

16. *Letters* 1: 265.

17. *Letters* 1: 189. He arrives at a decision: "Either I must invent a notation applied throughout as in music or else I must only mark where the reader is likely to mistake, and for the present this is what I shall do." Michael Sprinker, in *"A Counterpoint of Dissonance,"* 76, finds that the marks, in trying to recapture spoken language, end by proliferating writing.

18. *Letters* 2: 34.

19. *Sermons,* 129.

20. *Sermons,* 239.

21. *Letters* 1: 170.

22. *Letters* 1: 83. Hopkins continues: "The thought is that as the seabird opening his wings with a whiff of wind in your face means the whirr of the motion, but also unaware gives you a whiff of knowledge about his plumage, the marking of which stamps his species, that he does not mean, so Purcell, seemingly intent only on the thought or feeling he is to express or call out, incidentally lets you remark the individualising marks of his own genius."

23. *Sermons,* 239.

24. Paul L. Mariani writes of the breath/air/spirit metaphor in Hopkins' last sonnets. His article "The Sound of Oneself Breathing" suggests that the image cluster constitutes a "kind of ghostly presence" that may partake of the very act of the poet's utterance and so "authenticate inspiration" (17, 26). For Mariani, the metaphor is theological; the spirit inbreathed is holy.

"Henry Purcell" foreshadows the later sonnets, the creative breeze suggesting itself in the sounds as well as the words of a number of lines. In voicing the last line, for example, the reader not only echoes but enacts what the words are saying.

In his *Commentary,* Mariani writes that "Purcell does what neither animal nor angel can do, what the bird only fancifully does; he scatters 'a colossal smile / Off him' in singing 'his air of angels'" (140). Mariani so separates Purcell's music from natural motion, yet he gives the bird's metaphor to Purcell to do so and seems to agree with Hopkins' prose reading at the same time.

25. *Letters* 1: 83.

26. *Letters* 1: 265–66.

27. Hopkins' chiming wordplay and his habit of making sound more obvious than sense may recall Victorian nonsense verse. David Sonstroem explores a catalogue of similarities between the two poetries in "Making Earnest of Game: G. M. Hopkins and Nonsense Poetry." Sigurd Burckhardt's classic "The Poet as Fool and Priest" is far broader in scope, arguing that every poet in his wordplay must be both reverent and irreverent toward language. In its own way, each article comes to bear on Geoffrey H. Hartman's idea that Hopkins' view of poetry is "at once too serious and too light" ("Introduction: Poetry and Justification," 13).

28. Hopkins' definition of poetry consciously balances meaning and sound; see *Journals*, 289.

29. Howard W. Fulweiler, *Letters from the Darkling Plain*, 147–50. Fulweiler reads the passages more broadly than I do, suggesting that Hopkins was uncomfortable with the whole idea of writing poetry: "It is possible, even likely, that Hopkins was drawing with a frightened shudder a parallel to his own artistic career. Did not he himself learn an art of surpassing beauty and originality as God's chorister in the Society of Jesus? And when he had sounded that first note (the nature poems?), was he not tempted to prolong it at the cost of his soul?" (149).

30. *Sermons*, 179–80: "This was the process of his own fall. . . . as a chorister who learns by use in the church itself the strength and beauty of his voice, he became aware in his very note of adoration of the riches of his nature; then when from that first note he should have gone on with the sacrificial service, prolonging the first note instead and ravished by his own sweetness and dazzled . . . by his beauty, he was involved in spiritual sloth . . . and spiritual luxury and vainglory; to heighten this, he summoned a train of spirits to be his choir and . . . raise a hymn in honour of their own nature . . . and with this sin of pride aspiring to godhead their crime was consummated."

31. *Sermons,* 200–201; 201.

32. *Sermons,* 201.

33. W. H. Gardner first pointed to the *Aeneid,* bk. 6, where the sibyl introduces Aeneas to the underworld, as a possible context for the poem. Others have suggested the sibylline prophecy of doom in the *Dies Irae.* Coleridge had titled his 1817 volume (acknowledging authorship of *The Ancient Mariner*) *Sibylline Leaves.* References to the sibyl are legion; one suspects Hopkins was drawing rather generally on the tradition.

34. Gary L. Stonum, in "The Hermeneutics of 'Spelt from Sibyl's Leaves,'" considers the poem to be as "concerned with the activity of telling and spelling as it is with the knowledge thus achieved. . . . language . . . operates not only as a medium of expression but as a relatively independent . . . element in the poem" (117). But Stonum concludes that "language comes between the poet and his dangerous subject as a saving mediator. . . . Language thus serves as a kind of safe-conduct pass through the terrors of an apocalyptic vision" (129). Stonum thus reconciles by the concept of mediatory language the tensions in the poem, the drama that I suggest is in the difficulties of the speaker and his language and that remains unreconciled.

Fulweiler writes that "for a priest who defined his orthodoxy in the terms of the meditation on hell but who aspired to be a creative artist, the tension in the poem is nearly unbearable" and "the creative imagination is an illusion, which only makes greater pain in a world where nothing but the will remains" (*Darkling Plain,* 153).

35. *Letters* 1: 246.

36. *Letters* 1: 245.

37. W. H. Gardner notes that "voluminous" suggests both "volume" and "luminous" (*Hopkins: A Study,* 2: 312). Perhaps less intentionally, "end us" suggests "end dust."

38. William Joseph Rooney uses the poem as a text for comparing the structural and explicative modes of interpretation, the two modes leading to widely divergent evaluations. Structurally, he finds the poem severely lacking, with only lines six through ten unifying event and response. In contrast, critics who consider the poem as process declare the work masterly. Rooney's structural

analysis recognizes the turns I distinguish but finds those turns divisive and fragmenting (" 'Spelt from Sibyl's Leaves'—A Study in Contrasting Methods of Evaluation").

39. Hopkins marks each of the four uses of "our" with a stress; he also marks with a stress four uses of "two."

III. Bidding

1. *Letters* 1: 160. In *Letters* 1: 46, Hopkins names his own verse "oratorical."

Two recent critical works connect Hopkins' oratorical quality with discussion of an audience. Daniel A. Harris argues that Hopkins conceived of his poetry as part of his ministry, that he was writing specifically for a Catholic audience in poems meant to be *"utile* as well as *dulce,"* and that the sense of such an audience made writing poetry more acceptable to him. Harris' work focuses on the failure to reach Ignatian colloquy in the terrible sonnets. Jerome Bump, whose concern it is to relate Hopkins to a medieval tradition, writes that "the performance of the poem, the 'parley' between the poem's speaker and the audience, is clearly intended to be the delivery of a 'writ' for the audience's conversion." Harris, *Inspirations Unbidden,* 133, 129–44; Bump, *Gerard Manley Hopkins,* 69.

2. The poetry's fascinating critical history includes an unusual amount of subjective response—a fact that aptly answers a poetry that aspires to be "everywhere an act of intercourse."

3. *Letters* 1: 89; James Milroy, *The Language of Gerard Manley Hopkins,* 13–32. Milroy links Hopkins to Wordsworth in their rejection of current poetic diction and their attempts to bring poetry's language closer to prose.

4. An earlier version has far less tension: "God mastering me; / Giver of breath and bread" (Notes to *Poems,* 257). See, too, Hopkins' comment to Bridges on how "slow and laborious" a task writing poetry is (*Letters* 1: 136). Hopkins' 'spontaneity' is carefully wrought.

5. Wayne C. Booth discusses consistency of argument and emotionality as warrants for assent in *Modern Dogma and the Rhetoric of Assent,* 155–60.

6. Writing of the *Deutschland*, Elisabeth W. Schneider continues: "Where is the irony, where is the mask, where is even the thin screen of the impersonal that can lend aesthetic distance to make this a poem and not simply an unmodulated, moving perhaps but embarrassing, personal cry of longing and faith?" (*The Dragon in the Gate*, 39).

7. See *Letters* 1: 47, 85, 221.

8. George T. Wright, *The Poet in the Poem*, 22.

9. James Dickey, "Hopkins: 'The Wreck of the Deutschland,'" 842–43. Dickey qualifies his praise only once, and this, too, is revealing: "His world, his work, are tight and compressed like a spring; they are feverish and a little hysterical. One cannot read too much of Hopkins at a time for one cannot match his intensity" (844).

10. Emerson Marks, "The Achieve of, the Mastery . . . ," 105. See also Booth, *Modern Dogma*, 172.

11. See Wright, *Poet in the Poem*, esp. 24: "The poet thus plays a double role: through one persona he explores regions of knowledge whose laws are outside conventional speculative thought; through another persona he retrieves the first persona from a mere chaos of associations and employs the associations in a design governed by the syntactical and logical connections necessary to articulate thought." The tensions that Hopkins seems to contain almost by sheer physical will have made him particularly attractive to the New Critics, who applauded the difficulty, density, and tensions in his work.

12. The tension described is closely related to Hopkins' struggle against a subjective Romanticism. In "Hopkins: Towards a Poetics of Unselfconsciousness," Paul L. Mariani writes that Hopkins "was a rather extreme Romantic who, for the sake of his own growth, tried desperately to come out from under that condition, tried to radically alter or 'soften' his own ego, to sing the divine praises without dwelling so self-consciously on his own voice. That view, I believe, goes a long way to explaining his silences and his attempts to reshape his very way of singing. It even helps explain why the poet became a generally despised Jesuit, hoping by that gesture to move as far from the underlying assumptions of his

age as the Jesuits themselves were from the center of the vortex of Victorian England" (44–45).

J. Hillis Miller, in "The Linguistic Moment in 'The Wreck of the Deutschland,' " says the struggle again: "If the tragedy of language is its inability to say the Word, the mystery of the human situation, as Hopkins presents it, is parallel. The more a man affirms himself the more he affirms his eccentricity, his individuality, his failure to be Christ, or Christlike" (58).

For the reader, the poet's ongoing conflict with self emerges partly in the tension between the poem as process and the poem as product. Hopkins' forged features of language, distinctive and individual, push hard against the subjective unselfconsciousness and insist on the poem as icon, as product, but are also strong assertions of the poet's self.

Some critics responsive to the extreme submersion of the reader in the speaker's voice are Martin Heidegger, *Poetry, Language, Thought,* and *On the Way to Language*; Octavio Paz, *The Bow and the Lyre*; and Georges Poulet, "Criticism and the Experience of Interiority."

13. *Sermons,* 123.

14. For Walter J. Ong, S.J., close dialogue with another reasserts the uniqueness of the other; there can be no ultimate sharing or merging of selves. The nearer the loved one is approached, the sharper the pain of the inability to be as one: "The sense of being set off is not annihilated by intimacy. Indeed, it is heightened and realized in its fullness through intimacy because of the very interiority which makes possible intimacy between persons. As a unique and induplicable individual abiding in the depths of your own interior consciousness, you are in a way more other to me than even inanimate objects are. . . . [A person's] experience of his unique self is constitutive of his most intimate self. And yet it is this very experience that intimacy cannot share" ("Voice as a Summons for Belief," 97–98).

For another aesthetic which takes differentiated response as the center of the reader's experience, see Walter J. Slatoff's *With Respect to Readers.* Here, the deeper the literary involvement, the sharper one's sense of self, and "real respect requires not a suspension or withholding of the self and its full awareness but an exercise and offering of them" (90). See esp. 45–47 on the reader's physical self in response to the text and 49–56 on the necessity for distance between reader and literary character.

15. James Milroy writes also of sentence variation contributing to the poetry's effect: "Sudden changes between sentence-types— *statement* (declarative), *question* (interrogative), *command* (imperative) and *exclamation*, together with uncompleted, interrupted, and various kinds of verbless sentences, are very marked. Even in a poem of fundamentally simple structure much of the sense of urgency is brought about by such syntactic changes" (*Language of Gerard Manley Hopkins*, 198). Milroy's linguistic analysis of Hopkins' grammatical and syntactical devices, particularly the poet's compression, coordination, and repetition, defines the eccentricities of the poetry and relates them to speech.

16. Milroy links "Pied Beauty" and "The Starlight Night" in that they are both saying 'look at' and then subordinating a list of things to that imperative. He holds that Hopkins' language "is in effect a language of *subordination*" (ibid., 196–97; 204).

17. "The Imperative Voice—An Unpublished Lecture by Hopkins," ed. Norman H. MacKenzie, 113–14; 112.

18. The word 'redemption' has lured other Christian poets, most notably Herbert in his allegorical sonnet of the same name.

19. Josephine Miles cites 'dear' as second only to 'sweet' in her word count of Hopkins' favorite adjectives ("The Sweet and Lovely Language," 57).

20. Treasure is fairly standard stuff in poetry, but the repeated use of what is not standard, of the 'getting and spending' of spirit, may make the pearls, rubies, diamonds, silver, and gold in Hopkins (used with all their religious allusive power) more literal and vivid than they usually are. Further, by locating their source or end, or by playing an image through successive levels of meaning, Hopkins makes us see and value the gems afresh. See, for examples, "The Silver Jubilee," "Spring and Fall," and "That Nature is a Heraclitean Fire."

21. W. H. Gardner notes that there is no evidence that Hopkins had read Donne (*Gerard Manley Hopkins: A Study*, 2: 163, 172–74, 196).

22. Milroy writes that the interjections, more common to speech than to poetry in general, "reinforce the personal tone" of Hopkins' poetry and "help to bring about the sense of immediacy and closeness to situation and speaker" (*Language of Gerard Manley Hopkins*, 197–98).

23. *Letters* 1: 95.

24. Paul L. Mariani notes that the sonnet is "didactic" and that "the sestet marks not so much a turn in the argument as a mildly hortatory insistence on maintaining a proper hierarchy of values" (*A Commentary on the Complete Poems of Gerard Manley Hopkins*, 253, 255).

25. *Letters* 1: 187.

26. *Letters* 1: 221.

27. The whirlwind recalls the whirlwind from which God speaks to Job just before Job's redemption. The imagery of unfathomable depths echoes the depths into which Jonah is plunged before his redemption. The poem as a whole and its questioning processes bring to mind Psalm 130, "Out of the depths I have cried unto thee."

28. Howard W. Fulweiler joins Caradoc's soliloquy with "Spelt from Sibyl's Leaves" in his discussion of will: "Caradoc stifles the affective will with the elective 'will unwavering' in demonic self-mutilation or, as the Freudians might put it, self-castration." The sonnet tries to separate the elective will from the creative imagination and, in so doing, creates a hell. *Letters from the Darkling Plain*, 155.

29. Mariani aptly observes that the image of "dead letters" is "unsettlingly modern" (*Commentary*, 220).

30. Harris includes in the desolation of the terrible sonnets "Hopkins's raw and lonely recognition that, despite his assiduous cultivation of a surrogate fictive audience, he had for years been writing to no actual audience at all. . . . Hopkins suffered the discontinuity of his imagined society as a trauma only slightly less disastrous than his inability to sustain a coherent vision of the natural world" (*Inspirations Unbidden*, 142).

IV. Dramas of Time and Loss

1. *Letters* 1: 51–52; 79; see also 3: 379, and 1: 46, the defense of sprung rhythm as the "nearest to the rhythm of prose, that is the native and natural rhythm of speech, the least forced, the most rhetorical and emphatic of all possible rhythms."

2. Walter J. Ong, S.J., *The Presence of the Word*, 148 and elsewhere. My discussion of time and sound is indebted to Ong's work here and in "A Dialectic of Aural and Objective Correlatives." See also Victor Zuckerkandl, *Sound and Symbol*, 1: 201–47, on experienced time (in music), and 2: 202–64.

3. *Letters* 1: 46. Jerome Bump quotes from an unpublished 1885 letter from Hopkins to his brother, Everard: "the sensations of the eye are given in space, those of the ear in time," and "I am sweetly soothed by your saying that you could make anyone understand my poem by reciting it well. That is what I always hoped, thought, and said; it is my precise aim" (*Gerard Manley Hopkins*, 67; 72).

4. For work on the spatial frame of the poem, see Morse Peckham, *Man's Rage for Chaos*, 125–48; Gerald L. Bruns, *Modern Poetry and the Idea of Language*, 189–205; and Barbara Herrnstein Smith, *Poetic Closure*.

5. Hopkins thought carefully about the proportions of the curtal sonnet; see "Author's Preface" in *Poems*, 49.

6. I. A. Richards attributes to Hopkins an "asceticism which fails to reach ecstasy and accepts the failure" and says that "all Hopkins' poems are in this sense poems of defeat" ("Gerard Hopkins," 199).

7. Mircea Eliade, *The Myth of the Eternal Return*, 90.

8. Robert Boyle, S.J., has a thoughtful, informed consideration of Hopkins' time in "Time and Grace in Hopkins' Imagination." Boyle focuses on *Sermons*, 146, where Hopkins pictures Christ's passion as a river running through, and so directing, the larger sea of time.

9. See Octavio Paz, *Children of the Mire*, 11–17, which contrasts the Romantic and Christian world views. Paz finds the only universal ideal in the modern world to be change; criticism becomes an essential act.

In terms of the reading experience, Paz concludes that each reading of a poem is a "creative variation," a singular experiential moment belonging only to the time of the poem (162). Harold Bloom's theory of misreading also assumes that repetition of consciousness is impossible. Although most concerned with the poet-reader's "anxiety," Bloom recognizes that critics, too, must misread the poem (*The Anxiety of Influence*, 93–96); Bloom celebrates the fruits of creative misreading. See also Wolfgang Iser's article, "The Reading Process: A Phenomenological Approach," 285–86. For Hopkins, the impossibility of repeating consciousness during rereading is largely loss. See *Letters* 1: 79 for his shock on re-encountering the *Eurydice*: "It struck me aghast with a kind of raw nakedness and unmitigated violence I was unprepared for." The initial reaction is then softened by reading the poem aloud. Two poems, "The Beginning of the End" and "Confirmed Beauty will not bear a stress," speak directly of the loss inevitably felt when a poem is reread.

10. *Journals*, 101–2.

11. J. Hillis Miller, *The Disappearance of God*, 277 ff. Miller considers Hopkins' words on diatonism and chromaticism in relation to rhyme; a stability of pattern allows the abrupt change in each element of the scale of existence. All metaphors are rhymings.

12. James Milroy's chapter "The Wonder of Language: Hopkins and Victorian Philology" considers Hopkins in relation to Max Müller and other Victorian theorists, recalling Hopkins' remark that "'the onomatopoetic theory of language has not had a fair chance'" (*The Language of Gerard Manley Hopkins*, 33–69). See also Michael Sprinker, "*A Counterpoint of Dissonance*," 46–76.

13. Joseph Eble's article, "Levels of Awareness," reviews the widely divergent critical reactions to the poem before offering its own appreciative analysis.

14. Wendell Stacy Johnson, who sees within the poem the Victorian concern with seasonal time, notes the double meaning of "unleaving" (*Gerard Manley Hopkins: The Poet as Victorian*, 118).

15. I. A. Richards uses the poem as one of his texts in *Practical Criticism*, 76–87; for comments on "*will*," see 79, 86–87.

V. Recurrences:
The Wreck of the Deutschland

1. For some of the difficulties overcome, the ambitiousness of the poem, see Elisabeth W. Schneider, *The Dragon in the Gate,* 14–19; David A. Downes, "Grace and Beauty in 'The Wreck of the Deutschland,'" 143–44.

2. *Letters* 3: 135. Hopkins' father, it may be recalled, worked in shipping insurance.

3. Among the many writers who have explored the poem's religious allusions are Robert Boyle, S.J., *Metaphor in Hopkins,* 3–24 and elsewhere, and idem, "Time and Grace in Hopkins' Imagination"; James Finn Cotter, *Inscape,* 143–66; and Raymond V. Schoder, S.J., "The 'Carrier-Witted' Heart: The Ignatian Quality of *The Wreck.*"

4. See *Letters* 1: 44.

5. J. Hillis Miller speaks of the dual plot as "doubling" and writes that a "new experience of grace occurs within the poem itself and is in fact identical with the writing of it" ("The Linguistic Moment in 'The Wreck of the Deutschland,'" 52). Jerome Bump joins the poem to the nineteenth-century cult of the sublime but notes that Hopkins' response to the sublime is surrender, submission, and not the self-exaltation of the Romantics and others (*Gerard Manley Hopkins,* 101–17, esp. 115).

6. In "Newman and the 'Second Spring' of Hopkins' Poetry," Michael D. Moore joins Hopkins' theme with "Newman's own preoccupation with the providential drama implicit in personal, national, and cosmic events" (120).

7. Cf. the martyrdom of "Margaret Clitheroe":

> She caught the crying of those Three,
> The Immortals of the eternal ring,
> The Utterer, Utterèd, Uttering,
> And witness in her place would she.
>
> . . . .
>
> She was a woman, upright, outright;
> Her will was bent at God. For that
> Word went she should be crushed out flat

8. See Schneider, *Dragon in the Gate*, 29.

9. Of stanza twenty-eight Schneider writes: "The drift of this stanza, then, clearly is that the nun saw Christ's very self; and it seems to me equally clear that what is implied is a supernatural event, not an ambiguous 'vision' or a hallucination." Alison G. Sulloway, who views the poem in the light of the Victorian calamatarian mood, goes yet farther, suggesting that Hopkins himself had had a vision of Christ. But Cotter holds that miracles are not in question, Hopkins being too much interested in accuracy to have invented a miracle where none was substantiated. Schneider, *Dragon in the Gate*, 29; Sulloway, *Gerard Manley Hopkins and the Victorian Temper*, 184; Cotter, *Inscape*, 148.

10. Schneider, who discounts the idea of persona in the poem, says that "poetically" stanza twenty-eight "does not quite work" (*Dragon in the Gate*, 29).

Bibliography

Abrams, M. H. *Natural Supernaturalism: Tradition and Revolution in Romantic Literature.* New York: Norton, 1971.

Appleyard, J. A., S.J. *Coleridge's Philosophy of Literature: The Development of a Concept of Poetry 1791–1819.* Cambridge: Harvard University Press, 1965.

Ball, Patricia M. *The Science of Aspects: The Changing Role of Fact in the Work of Coleridge, Ruskin and Hopkins.* London: University of London, Athlone, 1971.

Bender, Todd K. *Gerard Manley Hopkins: The Classical Background and Critical Reception of his Work.* Baltimore: Johns Hopkins University Press, 1966.

Bennett, Joan. *Five Metaphysical Poets: Donne, Herbert, Vaughan, Crashaw, Marvell.* Cambridge University Press, 1964.

Bloom, Harold. *The Anxiety of Influence: A Theory of Poetry.* New York: Oxford University Press, 1973.

Booth, Wayne C. *Modern Dogma and the Rhetoric of Assent.* Chicago: University of Chicago Press, 1974.

Boyle, Robert, S.J. *Metaphor in Hopkins.* Chapel Hill: University of North Carolina Press, 1960.

———. "Time and Grace in Hopkins' Imagination." *Renascence* 29 (1976): 7–24.

Bruns, Gerald L. *Modern Poetry and the Idea of Language: A Critical and Historical Study.* New Haven: Yale University Press, 1974.

Bump, Jerome. *Gerard Manley Hopkins.* Twayne's English Authors Series. Boston: Twayne, 1982.

————. "Hopkins' Imagery and Medievalist Poetics." *Victorian Poetry* 15 (1977): 99–119.

Burckhardt, Sigurd. "The Poet as Fool and Priest." *ELH* 23 (1956): 279–98.

Burke, Kenneth. *Language as Symbolic Action: Essays on Life, Literature, and Method.* Berkeley and Los Angeles: University of California Press, 1966.

Christ, Carol T. *The Finer Optic: The Aesthetic of Particularity in Victorian Poetry.* New Haven: Yale University Press, 1975.

Cotter, James Finn. " 'Hornlight Wound to the West': The Inscape of Passion in Hopkins' Poetry." *Victorian Poetry* 16 (1978): 297–313.

————. *Inscape: The Christology and Poetry of Gerard Manley Hopkins.* Pittsburgh: University of Pittsburgh Press, 1972.

Dickey, James. "Hopkins: 'The Wreck of the Deutschland.' " In *Master Poems of the English Language,* ed. Oscar Williams, 842–44. New York: Washington Square Press, 1967.

Dilligan, Robert J., and Todd K. Bender, comps. *A Concordance to the English Poetry of Gerard Manley Hopkins.* Madison: University of Wisconsin Press, 1970.

Donne, John. *Poetical Works,* ed. Herbert J. C. Grierson. London: Oxford University Press, 1929.

Downes, David A. *Gerard Manley Hopkins: A Study of His Ignatian Spirit.* New York: Bookman Associates, 1959.

————. "Grace and Beauty in 'The Wreck of the Deutschland': A Centenary Estimation." *HQ* 3 (1977): 139–55.

Eble, Joseph. "Levels of Awareness: A Reading of Hopkins' 'Felix Randal.' " *Victorian Poetry* 13 (1975): 129–35.

Eliade, Mircea. *The Myth of the Eternal Return.* Bollingen Series, no. 46. Trans. Willard R. Trask. New York: Pantheon, 1954.

Fulweiler, Howard W. *Letters from the Darkling Plain: Language and the Grounds of Knowledge in the Poetry of Arnold and Hopkins.* University of Missouri Studies, no. 18. Columbia: University of Missouri Press, 1972.

Gardner, Helen. *Religion and Literature.* London: Faber and Faber, 1971.

Gardner, W. H. *Gerard Manley Hopkins: A Study in Poetic Idiosyncrasy in Relation to Poetic Tradition.* 2 vols. 2d ed. London: Secker and Warburg, 1948.

Grigson, Geoffrey. *Gerard Manley Hopkins.* Writers and Their Work Series, no. 59. London: Longmans, Green, 1955.

Harris, Daniel A. *Inspirations Unbidden: The Terrible Sonnets of Gerard Manley Hopkins.* Berkeley and Los Angeles: University of California Press, 1982.

Hartman, Geoffrey H. "Introduction: Poetry and Justification." In *Gerard Manley Hopkins: A Collection of Critical Essays,* ed. Hartman, 1–14. Twentieth Century Views. Englewood Cliffs, N.J.: Prentice-Hall, 1966.

————. *The Unmediated Vision: An Interpretation of Wordsworth, Hopkins, Rilke, and Valéry.* Rev. ed. New York: Harcourt, Brace and World, 1966.

Heidegger, Martin. *On the Way to Language.* Trans. Peter D. Hertz. New York: Harper and Row, 1971.

————. *Poetry, Language, Thought.* Trans. Albert Hofstadter. New York: Harper and Row, 1971.

Herbert, George. *The Works of George Herbert,* ed. F. E. Hutchinson. Oxford: Oxford University Press, Clarendon, 1941.

Iser, Wolfgang. "The Reading Process: A Phenomenological Approach." *New Literary History* 3 (1972): 279–99.

Johnson, Wendell Stacy. "Auden, Hopkins, and the Poetry of Reticence." *Twentieth Century Literature* 20 (1974): 165–71.

————. *Gerard Manley Hopkins: The Poet as Victorian.* Ithaca: Cornell University Press, 1968.

————. "Sexuality and Inscape." *HQ* 3 (1977): 59–65.

Knights, L. C. "George Herbert." In his *Explorations,* 129–45. London: Chatto and Windus, 1949.

Krieger, Murray. "*Ekphrasis* and the Still Movement of Poetry: or *Laokoön* Revisited." In *Perspectives on Poetry,* eds. James L. Calderwood and Harold E. Toliver, 323–48. New York: Oxford University Press, 1968.

Langbaum, Robert. *The Poetry of Experience: The Dramatic Monologue in Modern Literary Tradition.* New York: Norton, 1957.

191

Lowell, Robert. "Hopkins' Sanctity." In *Gerard Manley Hopkins: By the Kenyon Critics,* 89–93. New York: New Directions, 1945.

MacKenzie, Norman H., ed. "The Imperative Voice—An Unpublished Lecture by Hopkins." *HQ* 2 (1975): 101–16.

———. *A Reader's Guide to Gerard Manley Hopkins.* Ithaca: Cornell University Press, 1981.

Mariani, Paul L. *A Commentary on the Complete Poems of Gerard Manley Hopkins.* Ithaca: Cornell University Press, 1970.

———. "Hopkins' 'Harry Ploughman' and Frederick Walker's 'The Plough.'" *Month,* N.S. 40 (1968): 37–44.

———. "Hopkins: Towards a Poetics of Unselfconsciousness." *Renascence* 29 (1976): 43–49.

———. "The Sound of Oneself Breathing: The Burden of Theological Metaphor in Hopkins." *HQ* 4 (1977): 17–26.

Marks, Emerson. "The Achieve of, the Mastery . . ." *Journal of Aesthetics and Art Criticism* 16 (1957): 103–11.

Martz, Louis L. *The Poetry of Meditation.* New Haven: Yale University Press, 1954.

Miles, Josephine. "The Sweet and Lovely Language." In *Gerard Manley Hopkins: By the Kenyon Critics,* 55–71. New York: New Directions, 1945.

Miller, J. Hillis. *The Disappearance of God: Five Nineteenth Century Writers.* New York: Schocken, 1963.

———. "The Linguistic Moment in 'The Wreck of the Deutschland.'" In *The New Criticism and After,* ed. Thomas Daniel Young, 47–60. John Crowe Ransom Memorial Lectures 1975. Charlottesville: University Press of Virginia, 1976.

Milroy, James. *The Language of Gerard Manley Hopkins.* London: Deutsch, 1977.

Milward, Peter, S.J., and Raymond Schoder, S.J. *Landscape and Inscape: Vision and Inspiration in Hopkins's Poetry.* London: Elek, 1975.

Moore, Michael D. "Newman and the Motif of Intellectual Pain in Hopkins's 'Terrible Sonnets.'" *Mosaic* 12 (Summer, 1979): 29–46.

———. "Newman and the 'Second Spring' of Hopkins's Poetry." *HQ* 6 (1979): 119–37.

Newman, John Henry Cardinal. *An Essay in Aid of a Grammar of Assent*. Notre Dame: University of Notre Dame Press, 1979.

Ong, Walter J., S.J. "A Dialectic of Aural and Objective Correlatives." In *Perspectives on Poetry*, eds. James L. Calderwood and Harold E. Toliver, 119–31. New York: Oxford University Press, 1968.

———. "Hopkins' Sprung Rhythm and the Life of English Poetry." In *Immortal Diamond: Studies in Gerard Manley Hopkins*, ed. Norman Weyand, S.J., 93–174. New York: Sheed and Ward, 1949.

———. *The Presence of the Word: Some Prolegomena for Cultural and Religious History*. New Haven: Yale University Press, 1967.

———. "Voice as a Summons for Belief." In *Literature and Belief*, ed. M. H. Abrams, 80–105. English Institute Essays, 1957. New York: Columbia University Press, 1958.

Owen, W. J. B. *Wordsworth as Critic*. Toronto: University of Toronto Press, 1969.

Paz, Octavio. *The Bow and the Lyre: The Poem. The Poetic Revelation. Poetry and History*. Trans. Ruth L. C. Simms. 2d ed. New York: McGraw-Hill, 1973.

———. *Children of the Mire: Modern Poetry from Romanticism to the Avant-Garde*. Trans. Rachel Phillips. Cambridge: Harvard University Press, 1974.

Peckham, Morse. *Man's Rage for Chaos: Biology, Behavior, and the Arts*. New York: Schocken, 1967.

Poulet, Georges. "Criticism and the Experience of Interiority." In *The Structuralist Controversy: The Languages of Criticism and the Sciences of Man*, ed. Richard Macksey and Eugenio Donato, 56–73. Baltimore: Johns Hopkins University Press, 1972.

Richards, I. A. "Gerard Hopkins." *Dial* 81 (1926): 195–203.

———. *Practical Criticism: A Study of Literary Judgment*. New York: Harcourt, Brace and World, 1929.

Rooney, William Joseph. " 'Spelt from Sibyl's Leaves'—A Study in Contrasting Methods of Evaluation." *Journal of Aesthetics and Art Criticism* 13 (1955): 507–19.

Schneider, Elisabeth W. *The Dragon in the Gate: Studies in

the Poetry of G. M. Hopkins. Perspectives in Criticism, no. 20. Berkeley and Los Angeles: University of California Press, 1968.

Schoder, Raymond V., S.J. "The 'Carrier-Witted' Heart: The Ignatian Quality of *The Wreck.*" In *Readings of "The Wreck": Essays in Commemoration of the Centenary of G. M. Hopkins' "The Wreck of the Deutschland,"* eds. Peter Milward, S.J., and Raymond Schoder, S.J., 52–67. Chicago: Loyola University Press, 1976.

———. "'Spelt from Sibyl's Leaves.'" *Thought* 19 (1944): 633–48.

Slatoff, Walter J. *With Respect to Readers: Dimensions of Literary Response.* Ithaca: Cornell University Press, 1970.

Smith, Barbara Herrnstein. *Poetic Closure: A Study of How Poems End.* Chicago: University of Chicago Press, 1968.

Sonstroem, David. "Making Earnest of Game: G. M. Hopkins and Nonsense Poetry." *Modern Language Quarterly* 28 (1967): 192–207.

Sprinker, Michael. *"A Counterpoint of Dissonance": The Aesthetics and Poetry of Gerard Manley Hopkins.* Baltimore: Johns Hopkins University Press, 1980.

Stonum, Gary L. "The Hermeneutics of 'Spelt from Sibyl's Leaves.'" *HQ* 3 (1976): 117–29.

Sulloway, Alison G. *Gerard Manley Hopkins and the Victorian Temper.* New York: Columbia University Press, 1972.

Summers, Joseph H. *George Herbert: His Religion and Art.* Cambridge: Harvard University Press, 1954.

Thornton, R. K. R., ed. *All My Eyes See: The Visual World of Gerard Manley Hopkins.* Sunderland, Eng.: Sunderland Arts Centre, Ceolfrith Press, 1975.

Tuve, Rosemond. *A Reading of George Herbert.* London: Faber and Faber, 1951.

Vendler, Helen. *The Poetry of George Herbert.* Cambridge: Harvard University Press, 1975.

Webber, Joan. *The Eloquent "I": Style and Self in Seventeenth Century Prose.* Madison: University of Wisconsin Press, 1968.

Wlecke, Albert O. *Wordsworth and the Sublime.* Berkeley and Los Angeles: University of California Press, 1973.

Woodring, Carl. *Politics in English Romantic Poetry.* Cambridge: Harvard University Press, 1970.

Wordsworth, William. *The Prelude or Growth of a Poet's Mind. (Text of 1805).* Ed. Ernest de Selincourt, rev. Helen Darbishire. London: Oxford University Press, 1960.

Wright, George T. *The Poet in the Poem: The Personae of Eliot, Yeats, and Pound.* Berkeley and Los Angeles: University of California Press, 1960.

Zuckerkandl, Victor. *Sound and Symbol.* Trans. Willard R. Trask. Bollingen Series, no. 44. 2 vols. New York: Pantheon, 1956.

Index of Hopkins' Works

Index of Names